AGING LITERACIES

Training and Development Challenges for Faculty

Angela Crow

Georgia Southern University

HAMPTON PRESS, INC.
CRESSKILL, NEW JERSEY

Printed in the United States of America

Library of Congress Cataloging-in-Publication Data

Crow, Angela, 1965-
    Aging literacies : training and development challenges for faculty / Angela Crow
      p. cm. -- (New dimensions in computers and composition)
    Includes bibliographic references and index.
    ISBN 1-57273-642-9 (cloth) -- ISBN 1-57273-643-7 (pbk.)
    1. Engish language--Rhetoric--Study and teaching. 2. English language--Rhetoric--Computer assisted instruction. 3. Aging--Research. 4. Older people--Education. I. Title. II. Series.

PE1404C758 2006
808'.0420285--dc22

                        2005058903

Hampton Press, Inc.
23 Broadway
Cresskill, NJ 07626

CONTENTS

ACKNOWLEDGMENTS

I want to thank Cindy Selfe and Gail Hawisher for their encouragement and responses to the text throughout the process. I appreciate their steady support and remain grateful for the opportunity to create this text.

The reviews of the proposal and final draft were extremely helpful, and I appreciate the time and effort that both Ruth Ray and Lisa Gerrard gave in their responses. Their thoughtful feedback helped to shape this document. Also many friends and colleagues read parts of this text and gave useful commentary. Thanks to Lori Amy, Peggy O'Neill, Marge McLaughlin, Larry Burton, Amy Southerland, Michael Pemberton, Susan Kemper and many others who contributed their perspectives throughout the process. In addition, the people at Hampton Press have been extremely helpful and supportive; special thanks to Barbara Bernstein for her work with this project.

This project could not have happened, had it not been for Susan Kemper whose generosity and encouragement I have always appreciated and valued. Preparation of this book was supported by a training grant #AG00226 from the National Institute on Aging in Communication and Aging, awarded to Susan Kemper at the University of Kansas.

Finally, my family and friends have been supportive in the ways that make it possible to imagine finishing a book. I thank them for their encouragement.

INTRODUCTION
THE SEDUCTION OF CHANGE

SITUATING MYSELF

In Nadine Gordimer's *Burger's Daughter*, the main character, Rosa, explores her position as daughter to parents who raised powerful voices of protest in South Africa. Although her family taught her a language of protest, we come to see her as the recalcitrant backsliding daughter, not as interested in the continuing battle against oppression, unable to enter their symbolic. Bereft of family—her father died in prison, her mother and brother dead as well—she finally escapes South Africa and visits her father's first wife, a woman who had been at one point passionately involved in communist plots designed to topple the South African government. The first wife lives comfortably in the south of France, a daily existence without the missionary zeal, a less complicated life. Rosa stays long enough to glimpse that world, turns to England, lands in a flat of sympathizers, and encounters a man whom she once thought of as her dearest friend early in life, whose real name she doesn't even know. Although she has savored the memories of their childhood—mourned his absence, he remembers the situation differently, complicating her relation to her memories—causing her to see the complexities of any movement forward or backwards from the location of South African apartheid and her inevitable/inescapable location as white privileged activist. Shaped so completely by that world, horrified by her reactions to her childhood mate, her life changes. She realizes the luxury (and foolishness) of thinking that she can escape her family-determined role that attempts ethical change. Returning to work in a hospital with people wounded by the police, her actions are interpreted by the authorities as proof that she is her father's daughter, still involved in the cause, and she is jailed by the end of the novel. There, in the last pages, we hear her exchanging daily comforts with the other political prisoners, living more fully aware of the complications of eradicating racism, contributing in the only ways feasible for her.

Nadine Gordimer's story interests me because of its focus on generations and change. I often find myself writing cautionary tales about how change happens, full of hand wringing, worry, and, I hope, also compassion, texts that ask how we shift from troublesome actions towards the ideals we think we want. How do we negotiate entitlements that crumble, ways of knowing that come to be framed as perverse or short-sighted because of an inattentiveness to power and domination, to the sufferings we enforce, or the sufferings we experience—often without a critical awareness, an awareness that comes only because other voices find ways to speak, other perspectives demand attention, or shift the playing field. In the academy, these kinds of crumbling entitlements have been explored by those of us who are invested in moving from the "mythical norm" (Lorde) as dominating discourse, to a larger, broader conversation among people of different classes, races, genders, orientations, regional histories, religious affiliations, body abilities, ages, and kinship practices.

In the midst of desires to fix and mend and create hospitable spaces for those of us not historically accepted within the academy, we often fail not because we lack passionate zeal, but because we attend such situations in the midst of our entitlements, even as we try to wipe out positions of privilege, or we come without the entitlements; but most bring clear beliefs about how the entitlements should be disrupted, and the negotiations often break down. Given the complicated nature of change, the difficulties of eradicating repetitions, given failures and disillusionments, how do we hold on to beliefs/passion/intensities—and for my interests, how do we sustain long-term generational intensities that provoke change?

These are always my curiosities, perhaps because of my family of origin. I am the daughter of white missionaries from an evangelical Christian faith, raised in South Africa for my first eight years, long enough to be marked—South Africa, in some of its most evil times, 1965-1973. We lived on mission stations with hospitals, or in white towns/cities with large townships nearby. My family moved among white, Indian, and black worlds. On our shoulders, as kids, was all the weight of histories centuries old, of domination, of colonization, of religious, political, social bondage. Any photo my father took from that time locates that privilege on our bodies and the surrounding space. I look at a picture of my brother and myself each hold-ing sugar cane taller than we are, and I see the gender training, race train-ing (cars, running water—we have these entitlements because we are whites from the rich Unites States?), class training, the rows of sugar cane, the economic realities of workers about whom many have written. Dressed in our Sunday best, we lean against a car made in the United States—the backdrop a field of sugarcane, rows of cane in which I remember playing. Somewhere in the midst of this visit to a small community with no running water, we were served tea; gracious extensions of hospitality occurred. Although I know that my father and mother were not power brokers in mis-sionary circles, they could no more separate themselves from the structur-al injustices and no more right wrongs than many others at a variety of lev-els who tried. As a result of watching my parents, I understand that change happens slowly, with fits and starts, but I am not quite sure yet what kind of agency I or any other people have.

That I am familiar with a language of missionary zeal, of passionate intensity, of a desire to change worlds that are unjust, that my training in the Christian faith was a little quirky—I like to think that my father had a hard time separating Marx from Jesus when pressed—means that I have a language similar to a socialist training, that whenever I hear that kind of language, no matter the location, I hope for the world made more equi-table, but know inevitably the difficulties of such attempts. To escape exist-ing repetitions—impossible. To create agency, cleared of our own relations to entitlements—impossible. Yet this is a book about generations and change, set in the midst of composition studies, a work about aging litera-cies, about technological shifts and what may come to matter, about how shifting definitions of literacy affect our sense of the field, shape our sto-ries of hope, play out the language of my youth, and extend invitations to relation in which we want to believe we have more possibilities for equi-table experiences. This text centers on changing literacy demands and the challenges we face that are generational, that could be marked as aging lit-eracies. I also think this is a text about my own reticence to embrace the missionary zeal that I associate with my parents' generation within our family structure, but my inevitable involvement, for the duration, is in work that attempts goals similar to my parents' ideals, compassionate change that always carries the potential danger of colonization and enforcement of dominant ideologies. Although I am not Christian, I nonetheless worry when tensions feel similar to my memory of childhood.

When I say aging literacies, I mean three ideas: a literate awareness of aging studies as a field; the issues we face as we age in our abilities to learn and accumulate different literacies; and the difficulties we may face when we see literacies gain or lose value. Some of the issues I want to speak to in this text might be seen as old and tired ones for people in computers and writing, the first generation(s) who have dealt with these problems for over twenty years; that the same issues remain must be tiresome. Where have people been? I can imagine someone asking: Why don't they know about the different technologies that may radically change writing? Why are some teachers only now discovering the possibilities of hypertext? In 1994, J.L. Lemke argues that "there was a time perhaps when we could believe that making meaning with language was somehow fundamentally different, or could be treated in isolation from meaning making with visual resources or patterns of bodily action and social interaction. But today our technologies are moving us from an age of 'writing' to an age of 'multimedia authoring' . . . in which voice-annotated documents and images, and written text itself, are now merely components of larger meaning-objects." In 2005, I still hear people address each other as if the world of writing defined by Lemke remains outside the purview of writing classrooms. Someone like Lemke can say in 1994 that what we know as literate acts are necessarily going to need to change, but the university is a conservative place (Schoenfeld and Magnam; Tierney and Rhoads), and the pace of change rarely keeps up with shifts that are apparent.

Computers and writing faculty may wonder why others are just now trying to understand chat rooms. Why must we continue to define essays only within the confines of alphabetic literacy? What will it take for writing teachers to learn different literacies? The curiosity, for me, is in the interrelation of repetition and change, of the seeming snail's pace of shifts, and our locations from which we watch these progressions—how we place ourselves, how others read us, how we interpret the challenges of always changing technological resources. How we acquire these kinds of literacies still matters. That such literacy shifts require knowledge acquisition by a population that is often marginalized within the academy (Enos; Schell), gives me pause in terms of my own history and in terms of my collusion in the dominant culture's late capitalist agendas.

Nonetheless, what it means to write is shifting. This shift can be seen in the kinds of addresses given at CCCC (Selfe; Yancey), the calls various people have made to reimagine our relation to alphabet literacy (Cushman, CCCC 2002; Selfe, Hawisher and Ericsson), and in the attitudes we increasingly encounter at the local level. Writing faculty may want to learn technologies that shape writing practices, practices that they believe students need, but barriers may stand in their way. The role technology plays in day-to-day writing instruction differs by writing program. As has been noted in other work, writing programs are situated in diverse locations (O'Neill and

Schendell) with varying accessibility to technology (Moran 207). Many factors contribute to writing faculty's training and development, from technological resources to competing definitions of the field. In addition to these kinds of issues, this book suggests that if we want to accumulate literacies as faculty, we also need to address a host of aging concerns.

Faculty in our field may want to extend invitations to students that create the hospitable space necessary for them to explore relations to power, to speak important perspectives about race, class, gender, age, orientation, home culture, religious affiliation, kinship decisions, body ability, region. However, literacies change. To examine the intertwining identity shapings and the cultural pressures, to respond to these students' writings so that we shape and create a future—this is our challenge. That it happens in the midst of technology means that we somehow have to address the complications of our relations to shifting literacy requirements. Literacy accumulation for existing faculty is continuing and crucial, and aging plays a role that we need to assess. Faculty, after all, should teach the literacies that matter.

Our field has a rich tradition of establishing the importance of examining writing within the contexts of identity constructions (Brodkey; Cushman; DiPardo; Dunn; Farr; Gilyard; Heath; Hawisher and Sullivan; Kirsch; Malinowitz; Mortensen; Selfe (*Technology*); Smitherman; Villaneuva, to name only a few of multitudes of texts). However, our field has not taken up the issue of aging as a part of this puzzle, an identity category all of us will acquire, an identity that is pervasive with its own unique and important interfaces for writing teachers. Whereas theorists such as Deborah Brandt have examined generational moves, and other theorists have emphasized shifting literacies (Hawisher; Wysocki; Selber, Johnson-Eilola and Selfe, and many others), and still others have poignantly discussed different writing practices and technological tools as they affect their elders (Eldred), we have not explicitly addressed or examined how our own aging bodies (and others' perceptions of our aging bodies) affect our ability to learn and accumulate shifting literacies.

This book is focused on curriculum for writing and the role aging plays in acquisition of knowledge. Certainly, smart and challenging texts exist on accumulating literacies and implicitly address faculty development (from Brandt's work to the multiple collected editions of writers contributing to pedagogy and technology discussions—Hawisher and LeBlanc; Hawisher and Selfe; Selfe and Hilligoss). Writers within those texts address literacy concerns that can be transferred to this issue of aging (i.e., Charney). However, few articles/books can be found that address aging specifically (Crow, Ray, Van Hees); as of yet, we haven't extensively examined the role aging plays—what it means to feel as if one's literacies are aging, what it means to have a different relationship to learning.

If faculty value new literacies but don't feel comfortable accumulating those literacies, and if we can determine the role aging plays, then how faculty approach learning could be altered, because none of us wants to contribute to divides and gaps, to establish groups that can acquire the technologically based literacies and those that cannot. In addition to providing information on faculty development, this text lays a foundation of information on aging as it might impact rhetoric and composition studies more generally, giving us necessary knowledge about life courses, discrimination, and intertwining identities, about how our bodies change. Aging-studies information may help with curriculum design for writing faculty, and for aging students who will return to the classroom over their life courses.

OVERVIEW OF CHAPTERS

I have written this text as if I were in the midst of shaping a research project about writing faculty, deciding on the frame for that research. This text overviews scholarship from several other disciplines, because we haven't explored aging studies as a field. Before we can discuss actual research, we need a context that is much more extensive than could be provided were I to focus on results that I've gathered from primary research. Although my focus is on literacy acquisition for writing faculty, which gives this text a grounding, the discussion of aging research is designed to provide a researcher with a sense of what might need to be considered, were she or he to include the identity category of age in research design.

Thus, the chapters move back and forth between our field and other fields. Chapter One sketches out an existing problem—diversity of literacy competencies among writing faculty. With that scope established, I move to Aging Studies research in Chapters Two and Three, by first defining the category of "age" and "aging" and then by tracing some of the emerging research on stereotypes associated with older adults. I come back in Chapter Four to our field, to existing thoughts on literacy, and begin to shape some of the framework for applying aging research to the example—faculty development. In Chapters Five and Six, I return to aging studies—to gender and body changes—in order to add more information that needs to be considered when shaping research on aging. Finally, I sketch out some of the research available in adult education regarding aging in

Chapter Seven. With this scholarship and research, I move, in the last chapter, to a discussion of research decisions that reflect our fields' methodological traditions and the information available in aging studies.

Chapter One: This chapter marks out the scope of this text. I describe three literacy accumulation scenarios that raise questions of curriculum design/sequence, administrative hurdles, and individual difficulties. Some programs in this country provide leadership for curriculum designed for writing faculty, curriculum that eases their faculty's ability to accumulate new literacies; however, I'm interested in exploring the programs that are not cutting edge, and the possibilities in such contexts. Figuring change at the local level is complicated by many factors. Chapter One explores what we believe about literacy accumulation because our views affect curriculum design—from time allotted to types of teaching to standards that are established to keep people in or out. Although we typically think of illiterate Others in adult literacy education, the challenge in this situation is to make sense of ourselves as the targets for literacy training. Turning the tables may reveal much about our assumptions regarding the literacy training of others, but it also suggests the complications of addressing ourselves when designing new curriculum.

Chapter Two discusses the intricacies involved when defining aging. As readers, we may have varying levels of investment in whether we might be categorized as "older," "old," or "elderly." The closer we come to being considered "older," the more we may identify with those younger than ourselves. Age is a nebulous category. One of my friends, the doctors say, has organs that are those of a woman ten years younger than her chronological age. I find this fascinating, want to see the pictures of the organs (if it's not too gruesome), and want to ask questions she can't answer, as she doesn't have another body to compare hers to. How does it feel? Do you think of yourself as younger than your calendar-age peers? How would she know? If she's 45 right now, should she mark down 35 on any age questionnaire? Chronological age does, to some degree, play a role in our determinations of who is aging, but it can also be a somewhat arbitrary marker. In addition, our reticence to join this community of older adults has much to do with the social construction of value based on age. In a culture that privileges youth, being old means potential discriminatory experiences. Defining age also requires an awareness of cohort influences and life course expectations. Cultures establish trajectories for individuals, points at which certain accomplishments happen—education, marriage, children, careers, and so forth. How we see the life course, the narrative we imagine possible, is influenced by our location in history and the cultural values that shape our sense of a life well lived.

Chapter Three examines research on stereotyping because we may activate stereotypes about older adults that affect our behavior towards older adults and towards ourselves (when we are seen as older adults). This behavior can be detrimental to our performances and can have a significant impact in workplace situations in which younger (and older) adults expect poorer performances from older adults. Research from communication studies indicates that we will adjust our interactions, changing our speech and our movement patterns around older adults. The research also suggests that reminders of positive characteristics associated with older adults can shift our actions and improve performance. We need research that assesses the role stereotypes play in training situations because we could perhaps learn how to accommodate each others' needs without invoking ageist stereotypes. We also need to pay attention to the stereotypes we have internalized about old age and to our ways of navigating our fears about mortality, as these issues may influence our treatment of (other) older adults.

Chapter Four takes the power of images from stereotyping and the life course information from Chapter Two and starts to shape a research project for faculty development that I would like to investigate. I explore the relation between what we believe (or imagine, or experience) when we are placed in the position of not knowing enough, and suggest that we need to figure a way to shift the aesthetics we bring to faculty training and development, particularly when we feel like our literacies are aging and being devalued as a result. The chapter uses the example of a woman who listened to a conference panel that overviewed emerging technologies and leaned over to me and said, "Why do I feel like a basic writer?" I explore the possible relations between the images we evoke of ourselves as audience members and the learning we can accomplish. The chapter raises questions about how we imagine, how we think of the literacies emerging around technology, and how we position ourselves with regards to the technology and to younger generations. As a researcher, I wonder how we can encourage images and alter the role of audience members so that we can move out of a training paradigm in which individuals come to learning positioned in the margins. The research I'm interested in would try to understand the role the imaginary is playing in a person's decision to learn new literacies.

Chapter Five addresses aging and gender because the target population for my research example is predominantly women. Women's lives are often shaped by caregiving responsibilities. The long-term consequences of disrupted career trajectories due to child care or elder care become increasingly apparent as we age. Researchers point to cumulative (dis)advantages for individuals based on the culture's economic reward systems. Women's caregiving responsibilities together with the inequity in working conditions often mean that they face greater financial challenges in old age. Although many would mark writing faculty as residing in the middle class without these poverty concerns, enough research is available on the paucity of part-time pay in our field, and the disproportionate representation of women in that work force, to suggest otherwise. When a woman thinks she can retire has much to do with the life-course trajectory she has taken, her choices in partners, and family wealth. This chapter not only details the difficulties women may face as they age because of their life-course decisions, but also discusses the challenges that arise because women encounter each others' disparate life-course trajectories. Some women have chosen to put workplace careers first in their priorities whereas other women have chosen the value of family work, and tensions may emerge that are difficult to navigate. Not only are conflicts possible, but a woman may not be as interested or available (in terms of energy) to learn new material. In addition to life-course differences, women face other perceptions relevant to studies on aging. A woman is seen as old at least five years before her male counterpart, and women may feel the weight of cultural pressures for beauty, defined traditionally in terms of youth. In research design, we need to gather caregiving histories, assumptions about life-course trajectories, information about income, divorces, health care costs, and perceptions of others (students, colleagues, administrators) towards older faculty, because multiple issues may preclude the possibility of accumulating new literacies.

Chapter Six addresses actual physical transformations in our bodies (mobility, vision, hearing, and cognitive shifts). I compare Anne Wysocki's essay "Impossibly Distinct" and recommendations from the National Institute of Aging regarding web design for older adults, which allows for a discussion of physical changes and the difficulty of creating text that neither over- nor under-accommodates the audience's needs. This is a complicated chapter to write for many reasons, not the least of which are the high stakes involved in discussing physical abilities. In a culture that places high value on independence and physical ability, disabilities may be denied, but this chapter suggests that we need to assess texts designed for teaching, the effects of aging on individuals, and the ergonomic conditions in which teachers work and hold classes. As we age, our vision declines in terms of acuity, contrast sensitivity, visual field, eye movements, and the ability to discriminate colors. Our motor coordination changes, and may be more significantly different if we suffer from arthritis or other physical challenges. Our brains also age, and our working memory, text comprehension, and perceptual speed shift. Given these changes, scholars make recommendations on how to create readable text. Whether we like these suggestions or not, an awareness of aging bodies matters, and we need research that tells us more about how our physical abilities affect our ability to learn. In addition, training needs to explore the efficacy of various textual decisions.

Chapter Seven overviews adult education studies, suggesting some of the possible faculty development and training designs that might work for local situations. Given larger trends in workplaces that emphasize an individual's ability to be "flexible," researchers have been studying older workers and suggest some of the challenges/issues at stake for older adults' education. The changing global economic perspective impacts life-course trajectories, because rarely can an individual learn one skill and then maintain that skill over a career. Instead, people are asked to retrain throughout their lives. When faced with new learning, courses need to emphasize curiosity (instead of efficiency), or expertise (instead of a novice position). Researchers give recommendations about how to best shape learning situations so that older learners are appropriately addressed. The chapter encourages readers to think about the local context, the issues that may facilitate faculty training and development, but which are often not addressed—issues such as the creation of age-peer learning groups, or opportunities to talk about anxiety caused by new literacies. In addition, concerns such as space, timing, and proximity of peers to one another, are explored.

In the concluding chapter, I overview some of our existing research traditions with regard to the book's focus. Drawing on literacy research, and discussing research strategies, I suggest possible research directions that would integrate aging issues into our studies. The text is written to be both general enough that readers can consider issues to address in their own research designs and specific enough to show the possibilities for research design within the area of faculty development—an area that I think we need to attend to, especially as we all will face lifelong learning expectations.

SUSTAINABLE CHANGE

I work with my friend and colleague Lori Amy, who always advocates for radical change in this world, for shifts that might lead to more equitable/ethical living. You can see her determination in her body posture. To hear Lori speak always makes me feel like my research is a bit silly. Why worry over faculty in my local department, why address the gaps in access when all of us in this department have many more riches than anyone could ever imagine in other parts of the world? If I modify local strategies, what is the impact to the national or international level? This question: Why should I care about aging? I'm interested in knowing how change occurs generationally, and in the means necessary to sustain the possibility of change in the midst of shifts that are so slow in pace. Our identities are tied into the institutional, economic, and state structures that control the unequal distributions of goods and resources. Aging, like no other identity category, happens to us all and has the potential to bring us into conversation more fully. We all age. We don't experience gender similarly; we don't all experience queer life; we don't all understand different worlds based on class; but we all age. Granted, we age differently based on our relations to class, to gender, to the environments we can afford, but the identity is much more ubiquitous, and therefore, much more necessary to my agendas.

I also believe that the literacies we accumulate shape our ability to communicate in the public sphere. Many of my colleagues have rich histories and knowledge that will be excluded from possible participation in the public sphere when new literacies are required. In my ideal world, if we can figure out better means for writing faculty's curriculum design, we can raise a more powerful voice in public discourse. I cannot bring to the table the rich resources my friends and colleagues possess, people with longer histories in rhetoric and composition, people who have much to contribute in the midst of shifting literacies, people who will shape our sense of shifting literacies if and when they participate.

Not only would change happen differently nationally, but a focus on writing faculty's training and development can have local implications. I don't have any illusions that my work will radically impact the lives of people like my friend from childhood, living in South Africa; she was learning how to carry water on her head when I was learning how to sit still in church. But I do understand the importance of limiting local violence. When a colleague is trying to learn something, having difficulty, and feeling infantilized by the experience, I have a desire to help, to ease frustrations, to make the local setting more hospitable by addressing both the individual and the local systemic structure that makes such an experience possible. Knowing how to change things locally matters to me. Taking a gig at a school that has racial diversity, that has regional histories that are complex, I can work on contributing to the creation of environments that are good for students, good for faculty, and know just how complicated change is but how necessary it is to attempt different ways, ones that limit the colonizing feel, that eradicate the oppressions that exist. This local situation challenges me to understand how change happens.

I worry that advocating for literacy shifts plays into dominant ideologies, and aids in the larger globalization helping marginalized labor to continue scrambling to just keep up—a viable worry. I understand how commercial these literate shifts are, and how often programs change that make our knowledge obsolete. That attitude of always acquiring "new" skills seems fraught with problems. Nonetheless, in the midst of such profoundly troubling, agent-less colonizing experiences, I find myself enjoying the possibilities for communication. Certainly I understand the commercialism behind many of these changes in technological possibilities and understand that the seduction I experience is created by the advertising. Nonetheless, I want to improve conditions, blind as I may be to my collusions. I want to help people keep up.

Too early, I thought too much about how change happens, wanting everything to change radically. I think I'm still exploring that story. No wonder, given that beginning, that I have turned to age in my research. Age and change inevitably intertwine.

1

WHAT ARE LITERATE ACTS

FRAMING THE PROBLEMS

I have been curious about how to address writing faculty curriculum since my first year at Georgia Southern, when my colleague and I volunteered to conduct a workshop on how to use the networking capabilities of the computers in the classrooms. We found ourselves talking with a group of about fifteen writing teachers who were enthusiastic and kind, but as we examined possibilities for writing instruction using this feature on the computers, I had the sinking feeling that the workshop only reached a third of the participants at most. We had shaped the workshop based on our assumptions about our colleagues' knowledge levels. Afterwards, however, my assessment of the workshop was that it moved too quickly for the majority, covering too many new concepts, and we failed to provide adequate time to practice.

That experience made me curious about literacy levels within our community, about how much of a gap existed between our literate practices and our vocabulary, and about how we might learn from one another because I didn't want to be involved again in creating workshops that left participants without the necessary knowledge. Six years ago, my colleague and I didn't know enough about our audience, about how our own trainings and enculturations into the field influenced our perceptions, and about how learning happened for our local population of writing faculty.

For these reasons and others, we didn't create literacy training that worked. Since that time, I've been interested in shaping research that helps me to understand the factors that are involved in creating the possibility of learning. How should learning happen for those who have very little familiarity with the technologies that I take for granted? How should we sequence training so that the literacies are accumulated in the best order for learning?

People bring unique needs and expectations for learning that play into how they want to accumulate literacies. For all participants, the challenge is to understand just how much time, what kind of time, and what kind of information is required in order to acquire the literate practices. If we are to adapt and accumulate valued literacies as writing teachers at our university—in order to participate in disciplinary discussions and to teach students technologically rich writing literacies—we need to understand how to create literacy training that meets the goals of the participants; we need substantially more research on what works. To articulate the problems I see in writing faculty's literacy learning situations, I want to begin with three descriptions of literacy accumulation. These three descriptions may help to establish my research scope when incorporating aging perspectives into a study of writing faculty.

WHAT'S A LITERATE ACT?: USING E-MAIL FILTERS?

In the summer of 2002, one of the members of the WPA list (Writing Program Administration listserv) went out of town and set her e-mail program so that anyone who sent her a message would immediately receive a message indicating that she was out of town. Unfortunately, she forgot to change her status on the WPA listserv from "mail" to "no mail." Thus each time her e-mail program received a post from the WPA list, it would send a message to all of the list participants, informing us that she was out of the office. Each of her notifications then became a post that she would receive from the WPA list, and her computer program would send out another notification that she was out of the office. When I opened my mail program and found message after message from this participant, I clicked on the underlined "sender" option at the top of the inbox screen. My mail was then sorted by author, and I could quickly select all her posts and delete them. Another participant, an older woman (for the purposes of this example, I'll call her Mary),[1] who had only recently started speaking on the list, sent the following message: "PLEASE stop the [name omitted] messages: I just have received over 75 "out of office" replies. (August 1, 2002). The request was reasonable, but in my opinion also marked her as a bit of a novice (i.e., I assumed that as soon as the list manager checked his e-mail, he would fix the problem. In fact, within a short amount of time, the list owner sent a message saying he had already taken care of the problem and explained how to set one's subscription to no-mail). In between the time of her request and the list owner's response, another newbie to the list, a young man, responded:

> one suggestion for all:
> 1) take the time to learn how to use the filtering rules that are built into your mail program. (Outlook, OE, Netscape, and Eudora are all more than capable of doing this....)
> 2) create rules that sort all messages with the subject text "Out-of-office" into the wastebasket. they are rarely useful, and most often are simply nuisances.
> (this will greatly assist you in retaining your sanity. =) HTH, [Name] (August 1, 2002). (For the purposes of this example, I'll call him John.)

As I read through his suggestions, I tried to imagine people in my life understanding his advice. What's a filtering rule? How do you create filtering rules? "Angela, did you understand his post? Can you show me how to do that?" Based on my own experiences, faculty who ask me for help don't necessarily have the ability to apply the above suggestions. Thus, I would argue that John missed the mark for two reasons: first, he assumed too much familiarity with e-mail programs, and second, he believed that Mary would care (or want to know) about filters. Her message revealed clues about literacy level. If she didn't understand what was going on with a series of "out of the office" e-mails and didn't know how to move through them quickly, how would she know where to even look for the filter possibility? Although John might have thought this information was unnecessary, my own experiences with faculty in similar situations suggests otherwise.

---

[1]In Chapter Two, I will define older and age more extensively. For the time being, this woman falls within the category of older as categorized by the U.S. Census.

In my read of the scene, the two people involved above (and the silent third party who forgot to set her account to no mail) reveal disparities in knowledge: some of us are conversant with lists and e-mail programs, employing all the resources available to us from the mail programs we use. From filters to basic e-mail account set up (i.e., items such as the type of server—a POP3 server?), inputting information is automatic. We know our e-mail is an account and that we have a password for it. Others of us don't. We open Outlook or Eudora through a series of steps someone taught us long ago, and if the screen suddenly changes, we're not sure what to do. We don't know that deleted mail winds up in another folder (called trash) and are surprised when a colleague comes to help us with our mail program (the screen suddenly unfamiliar) and asks if we want to empty the many messages from the trash folder. We don't know that if you click on the word "sender" or on "subject" (at the top of the screen in our e-mail programs) then our e-mails will be sorted by sender or subject. Never mind a filtering rule. The gap between literacies can be large.

It's not only the gap, but the kinds of information we want to know. I remember being so surprised by a friend who interrupted my technology explanation about some feature in her program to say, "Angela, I don't want to know how it works; I don't want to know how my car works either, I just want them both to function without a lot of fuss." To contrast, I grew up watching my father write and then print his texts on presses that he had rescued and repaired. Writing, for me, begins in the technology— in the smell of ink and church basements, in the noise of language being printed, in the delight my father took in his projects. Others might just take the texts to the printer; I enjoy the whole experience, or as much of it as possible, whether that includes coding HTML or learning action scripts for Flash. My colleague and I clearly have different strategies, ways of knowing, and definitions of what it means to be literate in these rich technologies.

In the above exchange, Mary participated as a respected member of the community and functioned on this list at a level of competence that allowed her and others to carry on conversations. Should she know more about filtering rules? Would we only deem her competent if she understood the behind-the-scenes workings of list serv administration, or how to set a filter? The exchange raises an important question about what counts as a literate act, a fundamental question when setting up research on faculty development. What kind of knowledge matters?

Although my first assumption is that John missed the mark in his communication, another possibility exists: John may have wanted to enforce standards for who would be allowed to participate in this on-line community. I often function with the presumption that everyone would benefit from communication that includes participants such as Mary. John may not agree. Perhaps John was tired of newbie problems and thought that Mary should either become more savvy or stop clogging up his e-mail. Maybe he found her post a mistake on a par with someone who makes too many grammar errors and is judged careless as a result. John could be seen as governing the degree to which a newbie (who is not list-serv/e-mail savvy) could speak: "take the time to learn how to use the filtering rules" (*take the time*?). It might be similar to a comment in the margins of a student's paper—your comma splices indicate that you haven't taken enough time with the editing of your paper. Interestingly, John may not have taken the time to know to whom he was speaking, a comparable newbie error.

Whether intentional or not, the exchange also raises questions about identity categories—in this case, at least age and gender—and their role in a teaching situation. A much younger man instructed a dominant participant in the field on what she should take the time to know. His tone suggests questions about authority, shifting literacies, and age. When this exchange occurred, I immediately searched for John's home page on-line because I wanted to know his approximate age, what his affiliation was, his research interests, and so forth. My curiosity was based on research about senior and junior colleagues and potential generational conflict. Mary's entrances were interesting because she had not participated on the list until the previous year, and when she started, she revealed the small gaffes of someone who might or might not learn the ins and outs of list servs. It wasn't that she made many errors, but she didn't enter as a pro either.

That John stepped in, instructing from his position of young, male, graduate student was intriguing to me. I don't have access to what happens off the list—but on the list, for a young man to instruct an older woman was quite interesting, given my curiosities. Mary never responded to any of the further communications about the out-of-office posts, but one man thanked John, and another man took issue with his solutions. John jumped back online and reasserted his position. Mary remained quiet. Perhaps once the problem was solved, she no longer needed to waste her time, but I don't know how she interpreted his comments. For research purposes, one of the challenges is how to tap into audience/rhetor expectations and also to realize the contributing identity assumptions.

For example, in my own situation, age and position play. As a younger, assistant professor, placed in the position of teacher to colleagues twenty years older, colleagues often note the age disparity.[2] Although I hope that I navigate that relationship with care, I find the position difficult. The stakes are too high for each of us because I don't want to fail to meet my colleagues' expectations and they don't necessarily want me to know what they do and don't understand. I don't want to suggest only simplistic calendar ages in this issue of aging. One of my colleagues, also an assistant professor, a freshly minted composition and rhetoric graduate, but fifteen years my senior, has been in the awkward position of giving workshops to colleagues with much more extensive records of teaching. We are from a different generation within the university, coming of age (i.e., earning a Ph.D.) in the 1990s and later. In the second chapter, I will work more carefully with a definition of aging that will try to move beyond calendar years alone, but suffice it to say that cohort training marks one and adds a potential aging layer to this encounter.

Finally, this exchange raises complications because of its public nature. If local faculty at my institution observe the national list, reading these kinds of exchanges, how does that experience impact their local participation, their assessments, their expectations and worries with regards to the local equivalents of John—the ones presumed to know? It may be that a person saw that e-mail exchange, thought of asking what was going on, and then read John's message as helpful. That person might have decided that she could also post such requests for help. However, if she found John's post inaccessible, she might think twice before posting such messages and might be cautious in her questions when she asks someone at the local institution. This public venue may influence practice more than we might anticipate.

Primarily, this exchange asks me to examine my own and John's assumptions and beliefs about literacy. Watching and listening to colleagues, I have started wondering how to best address our differences and what help is most hospitable to us in the learning of new literacies, conventions, ceremonies, and technologies, particularly given our different tradi-

---

[2]Although I know that many faculty exist across the nation who are older and who have expertise not only in computers and writing but also in the field of Rhetoric and composition, in the kind of institution that I inhabit (a four-year university that grants some terminal degrees), I'm not sure one is likely to find as many older tenured Rhetoric and Composition/Computers and Writing gurus. I'm curious about local situations in which younger (and/or more recently enculturated) faculty are asked (or desire) to play these roles of technologically rich literacy trainers, positions that are not necessarily easy to navigate.

tions. I want to know the best practices because I'm curious about how change can happen at the local level. Although Lemke might well have predicted and addressed shifting literacies ten years ago, these changes are just starting within my own department. When the literacy gap between people includes individuals on the one hand who know how to program, interact with servers, shape text in databases and individuals on the other hand who struggle with e-mails, attachments, finding web sites, and using on-line courseware, I want research that attempts to find out the best practices for helping all of us accumulate literacies. These current dilemmas, I would argue, will continue to exist, as we will continue to be in this situation of facing aging literacies, though our locations may change vis à vis the rhetorical situation. I can well imagine, in twenty years time, being on the other side of the table from a youngster who is trying to help me acquire knowledge. I don't have to stretch my imagination far; students routinely show me how to create text in programs they know.

LEARNING MULTIPLE LITERATE ACTS

E-mail is but one literacy; the challenge for our field comes in the variety of new ways of communicating that seem to have arisen together and that may overwhelm us. For example, the Computers and Writing Conferences have hosted virtual conferences for several years, enabling people from diverse locations to attend the conference in an on-line location. Allowing more time than usual because it begins weeks before the "real time" conference, these on-line possibilities widen the potential community of voices. However, on-line conferences aren't necessarily easy to understand, especially at first glance, particularly if none of the features has ever been used by an attendee before. For this reason, each year prior to the on-line conference, volunteers from the community hold "how to" sessions on-line, explaining how the environments work and sharing tips on how to function well in the environment. To acclimated Computers and Writing faculty, these on-line components are familiar territory, and increasingly, as universities turn to courseware, a broader segment of the composition and rhetoric faculty may be more accustomed to on-line chats, bulletin boards or diverse e-mail interfaces.

However, several years ago, at the Feminism(s) and Rhetoric(s) conference (1999), this kind of literacy wasn't predominantly shared, though there was an on-line conference featured. Dene Grigar and her colleagues

held a panel to explain and discuss design issues, describing their creation
of the on-line space, which resembled a building—a conference hotel con-
figuration with different "rooms" for various presentation scenarios. In
order to create this on-line space, the designers decided on a MOO environment (similar to courseware such as WebCT or Blackboard though perhaps MOO advocates would disagree with this reductive comparison), in
which it would be possible to have chat rooms, discussion boards, aural
files, images, and video streaming. Although Grigar and her colleagues
demonstrated how the space worked and established the importance of
thoughtful architectural design, it became clear that some people in the
room experienced difficulty following the conversation. What was a MOO?
How could two people "talk" to each other on-line? How would one find
and then enter this location on the Web.

Whether or not my memory of the event is the same as what Grigar
and her colleagues would describe, I left that panel discussion thinking
about how complicated technological changes are for us as a field. In that
same year, were that talk to be given at a computers and writing conference, discussions would probably occur about the decisions made, the
strengths and weaknesses, and the possible alternatives, with people in the
audience who would have definite opinions about architecture, about web-
based MOOs, about strategies for video streaming, for managing servers,
for archiving materials. However, at this conference, the conversation was
much different. For many audience members it seemed that too much of
the information was new and perhaps daunting. With these women, (and
it was, predominantly, an audience of women) one could almost see the
fear writ large on their faces: what happens if we increasingly turn to on-
line communications as a means of discussing issues? Although many in
the room could probably participate on a list-serv, the very thought that
one would give a conference talk in an on-line environment might be troubling. Instead of answering questions orally, in the time following one's
paper presentation, imagine having to rapidly respond in writing. The way
that we want control over written text would become more apparent. As
the panel spoke, answering questions, one of these women, who seemed
in her early fifties, leaned over and whispered to me, "Why do I feel like a
basic writer?"

If this woman (I'll call her April) finds the technology overwhelming at
points and whispers something like "Why do I feel like a basic writer?",
what kind of work do we imagine for someone who decides he or she
wants to learn new literacies? At universities similar to my own, administration has made it very clear that faculty are to be integrating technology into
their classrooms, and we as a department must figure out what that means

for us in terms of program objectives and curriculum design. How do we shape the outcomes, how do we imagine the learning curve for teachers so that individuals maintain their levels of authority and credibility, and how do we create research that may give us answers to these questions, helping us to measure the efficacy of our various attempts, particularly as there is no one-time mastery? These are the questions of this project. I'm most concerned with how we might improve faculty development for those with years of experience and expertise who may not be interested in accumulating new literacies, particularly if literacy training leaves them feeling like basic writers.

Faculty may not have paid much attention at all to shifting literacies. Early on, MOOs and web page design (with html coding or now with programs such as Dreamweaver) were the points of difference. Other synchronous possibilities started to be available to teachers of writing several years ago, from chat programs to instant messaging, particularly in the form of courseware programs such as WebCT or Blackboard. Digital video and the accompanying computer programs for multimedia projects have become much more accessible to the average user, and working with these technologies allows for explorations of the relation of alphabet literacy to other literacies. Databases target on-line readers of web pages (think Amazon and the ways it personalizes the page when it knows who the person is because of cookies stored in the computer), and learning to write within this framework can radically shift a sense of text. Programs such as Flash allow a different movement of print on the screen and a different relation to alphabet literacy. Increasingly, one sees blogs or video logs influencing research in the field. Writers of pocket pc webpages or telephone "screens" are navigating the challenges that arise because of the size constraint. I think of the work involved in acquiring the knowledge necessary to communicate in these venues, and then imagine that someone is just starting in on these literacies—knowing that every year it's going to change. How does (s)he even begin the process? And where would be the best strategic entrance?

In my own experience, I learned the above literacies incrementally, and although I have different desires for learning in the future, I don't feel as overwhelmed as I might if I felt uncomfortable with researching on-line, making web pages, navigating the courseware package available at the college—which include bulletin boards, chat and white board possibilities, e-mail/attachment capacities, web pages, tests, and resources, and so forth. If I then heard a colleague talk about flash and how to create a web page that wiggled, with sound and video streaming, I might just give up. We don't know enough about what it means for a faculty member to decide right now that she or he wants to become familiar with the literacy shifts that have happened in the past ten to fifteen years. If I routinely were to create text with pen and paper, if my habit was to have a secretary type from my handwriting, if I never had to encounter a computer (and this set-up is still occurring, though much more infrequently), then for some faculty, to associate writing with advancing technologies means a significant change. When I describe this scenario, I'm thinking of a particular faculty member who is in his mid-fifties. He can easily be at the university for fifteen to twenty more years, teaching students in advanced composition. (Five of his colleagues are in their mid-seventies and are still teaching.) But one can understand why he might be reticent; learning various programs may cause a person to feel ignorant or ineffective or can be seen as a challenge to cohort traditions. In addition, the amount of learning required can seem overwhelming, given the range of literacies now available (increasingly expected and in some locations, required). Finally, the faculty member may not see the need for such learning.

In addition, learning is public—errors can be viewed by entire communities. An e-mail sent to a list by mistake is one of those frequent occurrences. If one has bad experiences with e-mail and then thinks about presenting a conference paper in an on-line space, or considers teaching students in similar on-line environments, one might not be very interested. How does one retain authority with a machine that won't ever do what a person wants it to do, where files can't be found, where things keep going wrong? For an older participant to make mistakes is potentially troublesome. Not only can mistakes be interpreted in ways that question a person's competence, which, we might argue are overdetermined judgments when the identity of age is added to the mix,[3] but the shifting literacies themselves may seem to undermine values one might hold that reflect one's enculturation into the field.

April reminds me that I often don't know what participants hear in workshops that I or others organize. If I did, I'd like to think that I might be able to figure out solutions to the gaps between what I'm trying to communicate and what someone hears, but it requires setting up research so that participants can speak to what they hear. We simply don't know enough. However, participants may not feel comfortable exposing what they actually hear, what they're learning. How do we shape research at the local level

---

[3]In Chapter Four, work with stereotypes should support this assertion—younger employees often assess older employees' competence inaccurately, particularly regarding abilities to develop new skills (in our case, literacies).

that allows participants to feel comfortable revealing what they do and don't know, in addition to developing a curriculum that sequences learning effectively?

Whereas the first example helps me to think about general definitions of literacy, this second example raises fundamental questions about curriculum design and the assumptions we may have about how people might learn. What kinds of outcomes would be determined by defining literacy in the terms above? What pace should be employed in the teaching of curriculum? How does one move around feelings of novice/learner status? What does one do with the public nature of this learning? Research from other fields and our own regarding aging and literacy may help us to shape a curriculum design that is paced effectively.

New literacies include on-line chats, instant messages, white board, video streaming, any number of courseware possibilities, multimedia literacies, database-driven web pages and documents, pocket pc web documents, blogs/vlogs, and so forth. Implicit in this list is a move away from an exclusive reliance on alphabet literacy; I intend aural, visual, and spatial rhetorics that explore different relations to time and are displayed in designs other than black print on a white page. When I describe these literacies, I think of people in our field who seem to create these kinds of text with ease. I also envision people who have trouble with e-mail, who have attempted courseware but given up, who can't imagine that one day they will give a conference talk in an on-line medium. Young and old fall into these camps; aging doesn't predict the ability to accumulate literacies. However, I'm curious about the role aging plays—the aging literacies, the literacies that may not be as valued any more; and aging literacies, the literacies we need about aging that may help us to better understand why an established fifty-something full professor might lean over and confess to a thirty-something that she feels like a basic writer.

STRUCTURAL INFLUENCES ON LITERATE ACTS

The above example expands the issues at stake in the first example. If e-mail is one of many literacies, what sequences, what processes can we adopt that create the possibility for change? A writing program may want to shift literacies, but may be stopped by the daunting tasks involved—how does one deal with participants who struggle with e-mail, who are not familiarized with courseware intranet capabilities of bulletin boards, chat rooms, e-mail, web pages, who would not necessarily believe that they could make i-mac movies, and shape program objectives? How does change occur in a writing program, in other words, when the existing literacies remain the comfortable literacies for teachers. I write this text believing that we cannot hope to meet technologically rich literacy objectives in our program outcomes if we don't develop viable plans for acquiring new literacies. Figuring out appropriate program objectives is also a challenge and subject to debate within the field. Defining writing and literate practices for our field is a familiar topic for the TechRhet list. After the 2002 and 2003 Computers and Writing conference, a discussion about multimedia ensued on the TechRhet list. The first year (2002), the conversation turned from celebrating different digital videos created by students in writing classes to questions about how appropriate and likely the use of digital videos would be in a first year writing class. Nick Carbone summarizes the issues that the group came to discuss:

> To what degree can FYC [First Year Composition], as it is currently defined . . . move from writing with words to composing more fully in multimedia? On a pragmatic level I don't think, right now, as technology, access and such stands, most FYC (think too of all the adjuncts who don't even have offices and some of the other conditions of labor in our field and tech. budgets in our classrooms, which are still predominately more brick than click) can move much more fully into multimedia than the essay with an image or fairly simple WWW pages and PPTs (and those are still going to be considered outer limits).

Carbone's point is important. At my own institution, with a faculty comprised almost exclusively of full-time writing teachers who have access to technology and could figure ways to multimedia compositions, we haven't yet created viable curriculum for faculty training. How does one go about learning new literacies? And why would one want to if these new literacies don't feel much like writing instruction? What if the physical space seems counterintuitive to teaching? How much does the training cost from both the perspective of administration and of individuals. Carbone addresses these issues as well in his argument:

> The pragmatic also implies a programmatic level, at least between the lines and coming from a WPA perspective. How would a writing program ever get this into a course/fyc curriculum and justify not only internally in terms of mission, staffing, training, and so on, but also externally in terms of explaining and getting approval for the shift from

other departments, provosts and various powers that be (PTB's)? Nick Carbone (techrhet listserv, Aug. 2002)

Carbone's question always matters. How we fit within the institution shapes our ability to change. It's complicated terrain, as Carbone notes: "If a lot of history, social conditions, shared assumptions, prejudices, material conditions, and so on got FYC to where it is now, the changes will come only as—and to the degree—those things also change." Carbone (techrnet listserv, Aug. 2002). I tend to agree with Carbone's assertions. First-year writing programs hold different values regarding computer-rich literacies, and their teaching practices reflect their ideologies. Our university, for example, has a commitment to meeting each first year writing course in computer-rich classrooms. I received my training from a flagship state institution in which writing instruction rarely happened with technologies other than pen and paper, chalk and chalkboards. In contrast, one of the local community colleges there emphasized the importance of technology, but faculty chose their technologies so that students might or might not have had access to computer-rich literacy instruction. This diversity of ideologies colludes with actual availability of technological resources. At some institutions, computer-aided classrooms aren't available for all composition teachers. A person may never have taught—and may never imagine the possibility of teaching—in such an environment (Moran, "Access"). Graduate students training in composition studies may not have the kinds of classrooms they need to fit the requirements of job ads that we run at our local institution; we expect computer-aided classroom instruction experience. At some institutions, the quality of computers in faculty's offices is so poor that the technologies demonstrated at a computers and writing conference in 1999 probably still wouldn't be feasible on their computers in 2005. Forget about learning new programs. In addition, training itself is costly, not only in monetary terms but also in psychic terms. Technology-rich environments within English departments still aren't necessarily a given. Teaching in the midst of relative riches, I sometimes overlook the disparate opportunities both for faculty and for their teaching situations. In addition, any university-sponsored training often takes place far away from the department (and from a discipline-specific focus). Space and computer availability plays a role in what people imagine possible. I also sometimes fail to remember that many faculty don't see how these shifting literacies matter and are not given the means to integrate technology into their courses in ways that are meaningful and also not threatening.

Not only is the question about resources a difficult issue to address, but this example raises questions about literacy, similarly to the first example.

To what extent do we agree on what literacy should include? Do we want to expect that first year writing curriculum includes web page design, chats, listservs, bulletin board/discussion boards, instant messaging technology, video conferencing, movie-making capabilities, sophisticated multimedia programs? It's not only that someone might say she doesn't want to know extraneous information when learning a new literacy (why should she know a filtering rule, really?), but our literacy definitions often function at the level of belief structures. For composition scholars, the definitions of literate acts are quite diverse. Although some would want to bring in these technological opportunities, and would see these acts as substantially shifting literacy practices in ways beneficial to writing instruction, others would view such change as disruptive to our mission.[4]

After returning from the Computers and Writing conference in May 2003, "Paul" started a conversation on the Tech Rhet list about the presentations he had seen that focused on "Flash, iMovie, and other sorts of not just graphics but INTENSE graphic design stuff in fy comp classes" and then questioned that move, saying "I started to wonder about the extent to which these activities are really appropriate for something like a first year writing class, or *any* class that has the label "writing" in it." Paul reveals an ambivalence that others may feel when examining shifting literacies. What becomes interesting is that he marks his fears of how others on the list will read him with a derogatory sense of aging: "we are teaching a lot of students to be really visually sophisticated but who still can't write decent paragraphs and sentences and (God forbid!) essays. (Gosh, that sentence makes me feel a bit like an old fart already (Techrnet listserv, May 2003). I want to hold off on discussing the "old fart" comment for a bit and discuss the issues of ambivalence regarding what it means to shift literacies.

I often think about what it means to write. Does a student learn something similar to a traditional paper about structure and logic if she decides

---

[4]Throughout the course of this paper, I will write as one who has come to terms with technological possibilities and has embraced some of these technologies. However, this embrace has not been without thought, without hand wringing. I've written and presented on the challenges and complications of shifting literacies alone and with my friend Scott Hendrix, and have found the rich information in the field, the hesitations of others, extremely valuable in shaping my attitudes towards and worries over shifting notions of literacy that occur within current technological capabilities. I'm most influenced by Charney, Johnson-Eilola, Wysocki, and of course, Faigley, Selfe, Hawisher, and others.

to take on a flash project, or a java coding challenge, in order to say something that wiggles on the screen? Is complex thought of this sort comparable to complex thought required in traditional print venues? I don't know, but I'm curious about the assumptions we hold about writing alphabetic text and how our beliefs then play into our sense of what it means to be literate. Paul's position raises questions for research. How does one figure out what definitions and beliefs writing teachers hold about writing; how does one determine, as a group, what objectives will be established that somehow navigate between national trends and individual positions? Which national trends will we follow? What role will research take?

In addition, Paul's comment about age deserves attention. By suggesting that perhaps he's being an "old fart," he's setting up a sense of change that relies on a paradigm of aging as decline. I would argue that we need research to help us figure out how to navigate the aging concerns at stake in the shifting literacies. An old fart is a troubling self-description for many reasons. If I want to question the value of a shift in literacies, I run the risk of appearing to be reluctant to embrace a change. That position of wanting to advocate for an older way of doing things is then equated with aging. "An old fart" is someone who doesn't want to change, who is rigid, who is "out to pasture," a stereotype we often associate with aging, and the fodder for discrimination lawsuits (McCann and Giles 167). In reality, across the discipline, older faculty and younger faculty advocate for shifting literacies, so what role is aging playing in this conversation? It's a difficult question to answer, but I find it a crucial question for research on faculty development because we encounter these new literacies in the midst of our identities as they are constructed within the university. Although a professor of composition and rhetoric might not have paid much attention to technology even into the late 1990s, it is unlikely that someone could maintain expertise and build on established credibility without having to learn radically different technologies that shift the sense of literacy. Increasingly faculty are asked to reimagine what a career trajectory might look like with new learning that may challenge our ideals. Technologically rich literacies can shift our relation to writing.

We may worry about shifting values in enculturation that may affect our abilities to maintain dignity and a sense of self, particularly if we wonder about our qualifications and our training and worry that we are not well prepared to teach visual rhetoric, movie making, data-base driven essays, and so forth. We may worry not only for ourselves but for our colleagues—for the disparities and inequities we see daily in the lives of our colleagues who may or may not have access to the same financial resources yet teach first-year writing courses and hear calls for increasing technology and shifting definitions of literacy through their worries and fears about how they will keep up.[5]

When Cindy Selfe and Susan Hilligoss put together *Literacy and Computers: The Complications of Teaching and Learning with Technology* ten years ago, they certainly understood how complicated literacy shifts are. In *Passions, Pedagogies and 21st Century Technologies* (Hawisher and Selfe) five years later, the questions about literacy and technology remain challenging—from corporate involvement (Faigley) and access (Moran) to the definition of literacy (Wysocki and Johnson-Eilola) and what should be taught in composition classrooms (George and Shoos; Kress). Many voices contribute to the increasing conversations on and complications of technology, literacy, and what it means to teach "writing." As these conversations have occurred, I have often been fascinated by how change actually takes place locally, at institutions that aren't necessarily cutting edge in their uses of technology, and particularly curious about the degree to which knowledge of aging might be necessary to any conversation about literacy accumulation.

At the large level, we could say that these examples raise fundamental questions about what we as a field will determine to be literate acts. In the e-mail example, one sees the challenges of learning these literacies. I imagine what it might be like to look at a screen full of messages and to have just one strategy—perhaps to open each message? Perhaps to click on each message and delete it, and then I imagine having some sort of mobility challenge. I'm not very good with the mouse; I can't quickly delete them. I might well write to the group and say, please stop! Although a (computer) literate act might seem easy to some, for others, these shifts to keyboards and mice, to computer bells that interrupt thought, to this screen that must be navigated through bi- or tri-focals, all of this can make the practice of sending a few e-mails extremely challenging—never mind the complications of making a web page and posting it to the web. If our literate practices seem to be fading from prominence, if part of entering the conversation includes the ability to play with many technological literacies, we may not want to participate. Although I cannot guess what April and Paul

---

[5] I am speaking specifically here of the disparities among us. I teach at a school with full-time writing faculty, yet we have different levels of education, job security, self-confidence, access to computers and programs, abilities to learn new technologies. At institutions with the labor divisions of part-time instructors, TAs, and tenure-track faculty predominantly trained in literature, these disparities may be even more profound.

intended with their statements, they mark their reactions/worries in two culturally acceptable associations—to be old or a basic writer in this culture is to be stereotyped as not quite in the game (Horner and Lu; Kite and Smith Wagner; Rose).

We return to the difficulties of teaching the genre/literate acts for a community, but with the added complexity of being used to authoritative positions. Aging plays a role in all of these shifts, not only in terms of having to accommodate role shifts at times when social clocks might suggest that we should be beyond certain novice moves, but also in terms of how our physical bodies shape our abilities to participate. We may notice shifts in capabilities due to changing eye sight or mobility concerns. In addition, our students and colleagues may interpret our bodies through their assumptions about aging, whether we are considered young or old.

Several concerns seem to drive these scenarios. The first issue is that of enculturation into the field, which can also, but not necessarily, be associated with chronological age. Research that examines change, aging, and in this case, curriculum for writing faculty, needs to assess possible connections between the time of enculturation into the field and a person's responses to current literacy shifts. What beliefs do we hold about the best practices to help students learn? What value does alphabet literacy hold (and what relation to other literacies?)? What are our definitions of literate practices? How do our definitions shape our beliefs about how we should learn what we need to know? What political positions do we hold on literacy? For example, if we hold a Paulo Freire "pedagogy of the oppressed" position, our answers about literate practices and how people learn will be different than if we subscribe to the Laubach training methods for literacy accumulation.

Second, the actions we decide on for our own literacies should be examined to discover if there's a connection between the beliefs we hold about literacy and the strategies we use to regulate participation. If we are instrumental in our department's writing program objectives, do we resist technologies because it would disrupt the balance we see between one literate practice and others? What happens between communities? How do computers and writing community members help/prohibit participation? How do rhetoric and composition members not identified with computers prohibit/help computers and writing participation? How do our beliefs about what we should be teaching and definitions of literate acts play into our assessments of what we are willing to learn? If we don't initially see the worth of a new literate act, how does it come to be seen as beneficial to us? (Or remain outside our desired literacy.) How much time, what kind of time, and what kind of information is required for individuals to acquire the literate practices? How do we develop literacy plans? What are the learning curves? What role does access (in an office, in a training session) play in success?

Finally, we need to examine the role identity plays in literacy accumulation. How do our positions on change and acquisition of new knowledge play into our attitudes/willingness (and how do our responses mark class/race/age, etc.)? What role do individuals' unique needs and expectations for learning play into how we shape training? How much do we understand about individuals and their willingness to adapt/learn in the context of identity issues—age, gender, race, class, and so forth. How do we understand missed communication in the midst of our identity locations, and how do we navigate gaps in knowledge? How do we find out what people don't and do know?

These difficult questions are raised in the literacy stories I've chosen to tell. These literacy stories are not intended to be representative and exhaustive of all the issues that a focus on writing faculty's literacy curriculum. Rather, they are the kinds of typical stories that I notice and try to understand. Clearly, they reflect my areas of curiosity and shape the terms of faculty training and development based on my ways of seeing the problems and issues. Like most researchers, I have my theories, my interpretations (guesses) about why faculty training and development succeeds or fails or putters along without much great success or overwhelming failure. In my research on aging and literacy, I want to know how it is that we go about defining literacy, how our pasts (at home and in school) shape our current expectations. I want to know people's beliefs about literacy—for themselves, for their colleagues, for their students—and how those beliefs shape actions/curriculum design/administrative—discipline decisions.

For my own research project, I start here: How can I gather up participants' definitions of literacy? How can I establish some causality between the beliefs about literacy and the issues that arise in accumulating new literacies? How can I bring together information about individuals who are learners, individuals who are teachers, and figure out the strategies they use to enforce their beliefs about literacy? And how do I shape that research to also address age-related concerns. These stories give a working foundation, a focus, for my research curiosities within our field. The next section overviews the challenges of investigating aging as a component of faculty development research design.

2

THE PROBLEMS
AND CHALLENGES
OF STUDYING AGING

[We] live embedded in a world of symbols and meaning, full of clocks
and calendars, cultural myths and histories, nations and deities, soccer
games and art exhibits. And the fact that the content of these worlds
of symbols and meanings varies so much from culture to culture suggests that they are all ultimately social constructions.

(Greenberg, Schimel and Mertens 32)

To define Age is to explore conceptions of time. We segment up our days
into measurable increments, marking time as naturally as breathing and
establish our place within the cultural sphere by the time we keep. A professor, for example, should be on time for classes, limit conference talks to
the time allotted, hold office hours, grade papers in a timely manner, and
so forth. That we assign value to time, that we learn to keep track of time
constructions is obvious, but the thickness of it, the daily acts that mark
time can astound. Expectations of time establish a sense of what a person
should accomplish within a day, within a year, within a lifetime. What
counts as a life successfully lived? What should one accomplish by the time
one is twenty-five? Thirty-five? Fifty-five? Should one attend college?
Should a person contribute to a retirement fund? When should kids enter
the picture? At the end of our living, how do we make sense of what we've

accomplished? At what age is a person old? As Kathleen Woodward asks, "is fifty old? Sixty? Sixty-five? And why?" ("Introduction" x).

A friend says that a full life includes raising a child, writing a book, and building a house. These goals may seem curious, but I too have a set of goals for myself that are shaped by family, by the University culture, by the influences of my favorite baby boomer theorists. All of these self-imposed directives are so clearly ensconced in the dominant culture's values. One finds expectations in the social clocks we follow, often without noticing. Our daily timed acts probably tell us too much about how our imaginaries are shaped by dominant perspectives that include our families and their histories, the previous generations' experiences, and our places of employment.

Aging happens within our frameworks of time. At the most simplistic level, we might mark age in terms of calendar years, but theorists suggest the complications of different kinds of time. Andrew Blaikie establishes "four axes" of time: "family, historical, industrial, and cultural time," which "form trajectories that interact to contextualize the ageing process" (9). A family might have traditions of long lives and might shape a life-course set of expectations based on a life that lasts until ninety. Their conceptions of time and pace might be different than a family that defines a full life as reaching one's sixties. How we imagine time, how we internalize social clocks may have significant consequences for faculty in training situations, many of whom may not enjoy situations that leave them feeling like neophytes. They may experience peer/cultural/family pressures to have finished with any new learning/education. Research should establish at least a cursory sense of the individual's sense of time pressures because our cultural, historical, family, and industrial influences shape our sense of timing at multiple levels of lived experience.

CALENDAR AGE

Dependency and old age, chronological age and the personal experience of ageing, social expectation and life course development have all been loosened up in such a way that meanings previously assumed to be coterminous and inseparable may now be distinguished one from another. (Biggs 5)

One of the first considerations in research about aging is what role calendar age will play in the articulation of "aging." Aging research has already established conventions, typically using four age-based categories: young adults (18–35), middle-aged (35–65 or 30 to 60), "young-old" (60–80),[1] and "old-old" (80–100). These seem like relatively simple classifications. A study examines the strategies of those sixty and over and calls those participants old. However, workplace research may set the ages for "older" earlier—say fifty-five (Kite and Smith Wagner). Given the government's determination that those forty and older can bring lawsuits for age discrimination, and given a traditional work trajectory with a person retiring in his or her early to mid-sixties, the determination of "old or older" can happen at a younger age. Earlier writings on human factors research suggest forty, following the government's lead.[2] The census bureau marks "older" as fifty-five to sixty-four and "elderly" as beginning at sixty-five ("Age"). These recommendations coincide with government-based supports that regulate and contribute to our sense of when a person is old. From this industrial/state perspective, studies of older workers might set a calendar age of fifty-five though these age determinations are subject to change. For example, in a recent study by Sara Czaja et al. participants were categorized as young (20–39); middle aged (40–59) and older (60–75) for a study on learning workplace tasks.

Multiple interpretations on what counts as old (based on calendar age) exist. For example, my predominantly traditional-aged, first-generation college students think I'm old, a status they informed me of when I was thirty-six. Their parents are in their mid to late thirties, so this perspective makes some sense. Although I was intrigued and amused at the time, their positions have implications for research decisions on faculty training and development. If I'm to understand how students read faculty and how their assessments are shaped by the culture—how they will judge faculty's work—I know that the category of "old" needs to be examined carefully, as the cultural stereotypes about people considered "old" play into performances in ways faculty cannot control.

---

[1] See Cruikshank for a discussion of the very names—young-old? Why the youth reference for people 60–80? What are the implications for research in "young-old" and "old-old"?

[2] Rife gives the following footnote in his discussion of age: "Government definitions of older workers vary according to legislative program and type of service. For example, under the Age Discrimination in Employment Act (ADEA), workers are defined as old and eligible for protection from age discrimination at age 40. At age 55, workers are defined as older and are eligible for employment assistance services under Title V of the Older Americans Act. Currently, workers are eligible for Social Security benefits at age 62" (107).

Although we might not think of ourselves as old, if our students do, their perspectives may influence what we risk in the classroom. Not only do students shape a sense of old that is different than my own, but the dominant culture teaches us to think of women as older earlier than we think of men as older (Kite and Smith Wagner). The current gap appears to be at least five years (Sherman). If I want to gather a participant pool of older faculty, do I mark the cut-off line at fifty for women and fifty-five for men so that I can more accurately measure this arbitrary age category of "older" (i.e., a woman who is fifty is really seen as fifty-five)? Given students' assessments and these kinds of culturally constructed definitions of age, should the age be lowered further, to forty? Or raised to the mid-seventies, based on research about when adults in their sixties and seventies define "old" (Kaufman and Elder)? The difficulty, as several scholars point out, lies in the constructed category of age (Biggs; Cristofovici; Cruikshank; Featherstone and Hepworth; Gullette; Woodward "Introduction").

Conducting aging studies requires volunteers, and researchers may have difficulty finding participants willing to identify as older, as even the women in late age (their 90s) within Carolyn M. Morrell's study were loath to identify with the category of old (73). Deciding to study a population of people based on their chronological age requires an awareness of these competing perceptions. In my own research, I don't yet have a steady rule, though I have often set beginning ages at fifty and older, despite the fact that I know few faculty who would want to be seen as "older" at fifty. Researchers in our field need to make decisions regarding chronological age, cognizant of the various traditions and the reluctance people may have to participate.

IDENTITY FORMATION—SHAPING A BODY

From this perspective the malfunctioning body can be repaired and the ravages which time has wrought eliminated, or held at bay. Both the surface of the body and face (the outer body) can be refurbished, and its capacity to function smoothly in order to provide an enabling, and preferably effortless and painless, platform from which to engage in life's full range of activities (the inner body), repaired or enhanced. (Featherstone 228)

Age demographics set with calendar age are one issue, but the actual strategies we use to make sense of our physical bodies are another significant concern. The study of aging as an identity category should raise familiar issues for those conversant in identity politics. We know the challenges individuals have filling out demographic information that requires identification of age, race, gender, class and so forth. What does a person mark if she has multiple race origins? How do we define class? What if we don't fit neatly into either gender? Who counts in what categories ties to the larger culture's ideologies and accompanying structural methods of enforcing values. To be marked as old has potentially significant consequences. In a culture that values youth (Biggs; Cristofovici; Featherstone; Featherstone and Hepworth; Gullette; Woodward, etc.), the inability to fit into the ideal, mythical norm that Audre Lorde defined as "a white, Christian, heterosexual, financially secure, thin, young man" may increase the likelihood of discrimination.

One wouldn't necessarily want to give up access to power as it has been established by the dominant culture; thus denial of one's age category of "old" seems a viable position. As Kite and Smith Wagner suggest, many people think of "old age" as "staying just over the horizon. While at age 30, 65 may have seemed old, perhaps it does not at 60. This has research implications when, for example, older adult participants themselves fit the researcher's category of old age (e.g., over age 65), but do not see themselves as old (e.g., they feel old age starts at 75)" (134). Significant reasons exist to resist the categorization and to decline participation in a study. Old age may be, as my friend Cheryl suggests, fifteen years ahead of one, but where we are in the aging process may also increase our reluctance to be marked as older and have more implications for some participants and researchers than for others. Researchers who are themselves in certain age categories may want to examine their own tendencies to select age groups or to judge age groups that others have selected. Kite and Smith Wagner argue that middle-aged people are part of a group "that overall is seen relatively positively" "yet middle-aged adults are also aging and so are closer to becoming members of a stereotyped group. This impending group change may increase their need for positive distinctiveness from older adults. In contrast with early adolescents, middle-aged adults hold younger subjective age identities" (149). In other words, whereas teens may think of themselves as older, middle-aged people probably hold images of themselves as younger than they actually are. At thirty-seven, when I conducted most of my research on faculty development and decided on the age ranges, perhaps unknowingly I was enforcing some perspective I wanted to believe—that fifty meant older.

The research indicates that our expectations for old include a reduction in competence but a rise in warmth (Cuddy and Fiske). These kinds of stereotypes may relate to the expectations we establish for ourselves and others who fall into the category of older. McCann and Giles note Mirvis's 1993 study, which indicates that "25 percent of companies cited the mental demands of work as a factor affecting decisions to hire or retrain workers over the age of 55." (167). We can understand our own or others' reluctance to identify with the age category if we will be stereotyped in these terms. In fact, age is an identity category with which it may make more sense to not identify (Levy and Banaji).

As with other identity categories, a focus on age raises questions about nurture/nature, about how much one can construct an identity and how much one's biological realities mark a category. We hear echoes in sayings such as "You're only as old as you think you are." Although each identity category has its unique issues and concerns, the reality is that the physical body has to be included in the theory because the body plays a role in the construction of difference. You're only as old as you think you are, save that we understand that a body's biological age contributes to a sense of what is possible. If I'm menopausal, I probably know (more) children aren't likely. Or maybe I'm wrong, maybe I can reproduce, given current shifts in technological capabilities (Blaikie; Cutler and Hendricks). But how much can we shift the reality of aging? Although the well-to-do among us may decide to afford radical surgical procedures that prolong the ability to be "youthful," modest or poverty incomes preclude others from the options of altering faces or skin and so forth. I choose the example of menopause on purpose. For women, this physical change is often the marker of entrance into the category of "older."

Mary Russo explores this question of body construction and the responses to those who attempt to work anachronistically—literally "against time" (21). She examines the construction of parenting, the cultural worries over women who have figured out ways to give birth at late ages. Citing the program *Dateline* that asks "its viewers 'how old is too old?' referring to the miniscule number of women in their sixties having babies with help from the new reproductive technologies," she reminds us that many women and men over sixty are currently raising "grandchildren and foster children" (21) and suggests that this worry stems from a desire to keep women in particular placements—"given the common placement of women's lives within the symbolic confines of birth, reproduction, and death, the risk of anachronism is scandal" (21). Those of us who made our way through texts such as Judith Butler's *Gender Trouble* and *Bodies that Matter* recognize that bodies come to matter through cultural constructions. As Butler argues, "gender is an identity tenuously constituted in time, instituted in an exterior space through a stylized repetition of acts" (*Gender*

Trouble). Those stylized repetitions of acts accrue and challenge the idea that one can easily shift a body and the read of that body. A woman who wants to construct her body differently faces risks. People marked as older may feel enormous pressures to limit what they imagine as possible; thus, resisting the category makes sense. Research should pay attention to how individuals understand their identity in terms of aging and in terms of others' perceptions.

COHORT

Did the movement from the old GDR to a united Germany have more profound effects among retired officers who lost more than a third of their pension income, midadult single mothers who no longer had support guarantee through social policy, or young people who found that their Ph.D. diplomas were not worth the paper on which they were engraved? (Hagestad and Dannefer 8)

Because calendar age determinations alone are inadequate, other factors matter when conducting research, such as cohort analysis. A population of faculty over fifty were born as early as the 1930s and as late as the early 1950s. Part of that group would be comprised of baby boomers and part would include people who were children during World War II. One doesn't have to stray far to hear generalizations about these groups. Although each cohort would have lived through "the women's movement, the sexual revolution, the Vietnam War, the popularity of the counterculture and the drug culture, and the civil rights movement" (Scott 367), their perceptions of these events would be, to some degree, shaped by their ages at the time at which these events occurred. Understanding their life trajectories means knowing when and where they came of age and how they reacted to the radically shifting times. Even within a cohort category like the baby boomers, "rapid social changes . . . have created different experiences between the youngest and the oldest of the baby boomers" (Scott).

To some degree, focusing on cohort can give us useful information. Take, for example, Ruth E. Ray's discussion on methodology in aging. She relies on some general experiences among cohorts that, she would argue, shape their perspectives and ways of living:

Compared to our mothers' and grandmothers' generations, we have married later, had fewer children, and had them later in life. Although

more women are working for pay outside the home, we are not as
financially secure as our parents were in their middle age; we have
saved less and borrowed more; and we have not planned prudently for
our retirement. (117)

Ray is careful to acknowledge that generational "members vary in the
degree to which they rely on generational culture to establish individual
identity," and she suggests the consequences of cohort influence when one
examines feminist academics' ways of making senses; we may characterize one another and dismiss one another, because we have been shaped by
our time of training in the university:

> Third-wave feminists—those academically trained in the late 1980s
> and 1990s—have been characterized by second-wave feminists as the-
> oretically obsessed careerists who avoid grassroots activism. Second-
> wave feminists—those academically trained in the late 1960s through
> the early 1980s—are often characterized by third wavers as "old social
> activists" who are out of touch with the latest theories. (118)

These arguments suggest a need to be aware of generational cohort characterizations and their impact. Baby boomer theorists, and Generation
Xers may be in conflict with one another because our cohort experiences
shape our values both in terms of our formal education and our experience
of the world.

The general inclination to make sense of cohorts needs to be tempered. As Margaret Morganroth Gullette warns us, cohort generalizations
can be dangerous: "being 'an X-er or an aging boomer can seem more significant than being, say, a woman, Chinese-American, or gay to the person
in question" ("Age Studies" 215). In addition, attributing behaviors to
cohorts can mask larger economic issues: the "Bush recession that left
young people without jobs" resulted, according to Gullette, in characterizations of the Generation X population as slackers: "The media took on the
responsibility of muting sympathy and resistance by hinting that the vic-
tims didn't want to work hard enough; this also disciplined those who had
jobs" (226). When a "growth of jobs" occurred, the media then spent
"years recharacterizing the X-ers as valuable members of society" (226).
"What is hidden" she reminds us, "was the decline in good and secure jobs
for people in their middle years as well as the young. Economic history was
disguised as generational rivalry" (226). Whereas cohort information can
help to shape chronological age and is dependent on calendar time, one

must assess patterns carefully, looking for other clues—individual, cultural, economical, and so forth—for why a person behaves as he or she does. In addition, age-cohorts don't necessarily attend graduate school at the same time. Someone in her fifties may share more educational enculturations with a thirty-something colleague because they earned their PhDs at the same time. One has to be careful to check for multiple cohort possibilities.

How one selects an aging population remains challenging. Is chronological age enough? Or should chronological age be mixed with identity perceptions? How do we determine the role of cohort? These difficult questions are further complicated when adding in the issues associated with life course studies.

LIFE COURSE CONCERNS

A narrative approach to development acknowledges the interconnectedness of individual and cultural narratives. Individual life narratives are situated within a myriad of overlapping familial, religious, socioeconomic and cultural contexts. The narrative of any individual life is an expression of, an embodiment of, these contexts and systems of meaning within which it is lived. In this sense a narrative orientation to development is radically contextual. (Rossiter 65)

Calendar age and individuals' ways of making sense of their aging identities are complicated enough to untangle, but added to these issues is the challenge of understanding life-course theories and the impact of these traditions on research as a result. Take, for example, my brother Greg, and my friend Jane. Greg would fit into a traditional life-course trajectory of the typical middle-class, white male. He attended college at precisely the expected age, earned his PhD in theoretical mathematics in his late twenties; with his wife, who is a medical doctor, they are raising three kids. A full professor before he reached age forty, I'm guessing that he will retire in his late fifties/early sixties. He's financially secure, thin, white, heterosexual, Christian, able bodied, the poster child for a certain set of assumptions about how a life proceeds. My friend Jane also fits into certain life course and social-clock expectations for women who came of age in the midst of historical change that opened opportunities for women. She married a man when they were both young, after college in the late 1950s; they had three kids and she worked as a teacher. Returning to the university in the

1970s and earning a masters degree, she taught at a community college and then earned her PhD in composition and rhetoric in her fifties following her divorce. She began a tenure-track job at a university in her late fifties, about the age my brother will likely retire. She, too, fits a certain paradigm of life-course shifts for white middle-class women of her cohort. However, imagine for a moment that Greg and Jane are currently fifty-seven and in the same field—Writing Studies—for the purposes of this issue of aging and selection of research subjects. Jane has just started at the institution where Greg has worked for thirty years. Greg has one year left; Jane intends to stay as long as possible, feasibly there into her mid to late seventies. Jane is recently enculturated into the discipline; Greg has increasingly moved towards administrative duties and away from the field of origin. Given their different life course trajectories, how will they approach new literacy training?

Increasingly, individuals follow more loosely defined life courses (Biggs; Cristofovici; Ferraro; Gullette; Henretta; Howell, Carter, and Schied; Kressley and Huebschmann; Moen; Ray; Settersten and Lovegreen). My brother's anticipated trajectory has a rising and a falling action with regards to work. Although Greg may hope to work at another position after he retires, his sense of when one establishes a career, how long one stays in a position, and what one does after one retires follow a trajectory, of winding up and then winding down. Similarly, Jane has also kept a sense of a life trajectory though the pace and the expectations are different. Her's considered a paid job secondary to the unpaid work of raising children. After the raising of children, she returned for her PhD and her paid career started gathering a certain kind of steam at the chronological age at which my brother's career is finished.

Both Jane and Greg fit patterns of gendered stories available from life course theorists. Simon Biggs argues that "the theories" we adopt to make sense of our development are "potential frameworks" for interpreting events in our lives: "midlife, for example, may be presented as a new beginning or as an adjustment to decline" (14). The theories "influence the stories people tell themselves about their own and others' life experience" (14). Life course expectations and trajectories are studied in both sociology and psychology. Although the two fields have different emphases, they both have tended toward a tradition of a "tripartite division of the life-course into education, employment, and retirement segments" (114), but each has increasingly moved to a sense of the life course as more flexible, with blurred boundaries regarding stages. The sociologists would perhaps emphasize the connection between our life course story shifts and economic necessities of a global economy. Whatever the causes of more loosely defined life course trajectories, an overview of life-course traditions may help to establish the challenges of shaping age-related research.

ERIKSON AND JUNG'S
LIFE COURSE PERSPECTIVES

Frameworks for life course discussions in psychology often begin with a comparison of Erikson and Jung. Each articulated significant developmental patterns in a life related to chronological age (and to gender). Erik Erikson proposed eight stages to life, five of which happen before a person turns 19. Of the remaining three stages, each covers about 20 years, leaving the last stage to start at 65 (Erikson 247-69). Erikson's stages emphasize early life, and the difficulty with his theory is that one doesn't have many tasks in adulthood: "the core tensions that have to be resolved are between generativity and stagnation" and "in old age, tension is said to exist between integrity on the one hand and disgust and despair on the other" (29). Biggs critiques Erikson's model because "each stage, at least in mid and late adulthood, is essentially empty of meaning" (34).

Rising action and falling action are in some ways the agendas of these traditional frameworks. In contrast to Erikson, Jung places the rising action in the second half of life. In Jung's two parts of life, the first half (until about age 40) is characterized as a time when "the ego gains increasing mastery (Helson 22) and the second half as a time when "people begin to question their commitments" (22). In the first half, the individual learns how to adapt to "the demands of her or his social environment" (Biggs 40), whereas in the second half the agenda is something Jung describes as "individuation," the process by which one establishes distinctions from others. Rebecca A. Parker and Carolyn M. Aldwin suggest that midlife is a time when "the long-suppressed animus demands expression" (67). A woman who has spent her life in her house might have increased interest "in achievement and accomplishments, especially outside the home," whereas a person who has focused on competition and achievement outside the home might become more interested in "familial and nurturant concerns" (67).

In these versions, the gendered issues are paramount (and also the subject of Chapter Five's discussion about untangling identity categories). Although Jung establishes a major shift at 40, his agendas remain concerned with education, family, and retirement or the adjustment to a persona that fits with the stresses and pressures of the life course expectations. Although his "key propositions and constructs have been elusive and difficult to test" (Lachman and James "Charting" 7), these early assertions suggest a desire to predict life. We somehow want to delineate the stages of a person's life despite extensive variables.

In contrast with these early theories, Ravenna Helson reminds readers that stages in life can be "influenced by factors affecting the opportunity for growth and self expansion, such as social class, gender, and cohort" (25). Based on research, people experience "a period of industriousness in their 30s, accentuated striving and readjustments of various sorts between their late 30s and late 40s, and responsibility and stability in their 50s" (25). The fifties are often marked as a 'decade of reminders,' in which one's everyday encounters convey the information that one is considered an old-timer" (Helson 28).

While Helson suggests this narrative of decline, others are defining middle-age as a time that extends as long as possible, if not indefinitely (Biggs 51; Hockey and James 87; Katz 70; Sawchuck 174, 179). In part, the rise of a "third age" may be a way of blurring the tripartite view, a move that may reflect a desire to erase a "retired" or "older" image of the self. Peter Laslett's solution to rising/falling action debates is to extend the rising action indefinitely, prolonging a third age. He describes four ages: the first age, marked by "dependence, socialization, immaturity and education"; the second age of "independence, maturity and responsibility, of earning and of saving"; the third age "of personal fulfillment" and finally the fourth age of "dependence, decrepitude, and death" (4). This shift enables the time one is in the category of the "third age" to expand beyond the limits of a midlife. The implications of a third age, one that can extend to the very tail end of a life span, means that one could be feasibly in one's eighties and fit within the third age, thus creating research challenges. How do people see themselves in the life course trajectory? Are they "older" or "elderly" as the census indicates? Or are they in some nebulous terrain of a "third age"? What does one make of a time period for development that could last from 35–85?

The consequence of an extended third age is two-fold. First, the category of "old" is reserved for near death. Whereas typically the category of old begins at around sixty, the idea of a prolonged "third age" attempts in some ways to negate the ability to mark out the territory of aging. The second consequence is that "deep old age . . . suffers from yet more distancing, stigmatization, and denial. Positive ageing is in part a response to population ageing by marketers anxious to stimulate demand" (22), but "stronger taboos form around those in poverty, those whose pastimes lack positive cultural resonances, and those suffering from disability and diseases such as Alzheimer's" (23). This strategy of a "third age" makes sense, given the cultural taboos associated with deep old age—taboos that represent our fear of mortality and the discriminatory effects of stereotypes associated with old age.

These life courses often are shaped based on larger market conditions, and sociologists attempt to integrate the individual's decisions into the larger social, political, and economic spheres (Hagestad and Dannefer, 4). As Moen indicates, "the life course has been organized and regulated in terms of paid work" (181), and as Henretta proposes the life course "tripartite division" "is produced by the institutions surrounding employment and the welfare state that produce regular, age-related transitions from one segment to another" (258). This emphasis on industrial components is echoed in Angela O'Rand's writing when she maintains that "in advanced technological societies dominated by strong market institutions and weak welfare systems, the conversion of family capital into human capital and, in turn, of human capital into economic capital that can be exchanged for health maintenance and a better quality of life are the central tasks of the life course" (19). Although she contends that "these tasks are anchored to deep evolutionary processes that underlie the human life course," she also links these tasks to the larger industrial structures: these tasks "are also socially defined by institutional arrangements that produce inequalities within aging cohorts" (19). To study life courses, then, from a sociological perspective is to explore what Haraven calls "three types of timing": "individual timing of life transitions in relation to historical events; synchronization of individual and family life transitions under varying historical and cultural contexts; and the impact of earlier life events, as shaped by historical and cultural contexts; and the impact of earlier life events, as shaped by historical circumstances on subsequent ones" (142).

Although the traditional tripartite of a life course might work for the likes of my brother, the tripartite structure doesn't seem to function for many current attempts to figure out viable life course directions. In part, these frames aren't working because so much has changed within the economy, as Haraven acknowledges: "Since the 1980s, more erratic and flexible patterns in the timing of life-course transitions have appeared again" (146). Attributing causes to such erratic patterns lead Cutler and Hendricks to point to shifts to global economies. "Formerly, once policies were in place and personal attitudes or characteristics, such as health status, were congruent, local economies and demographics were significant as far as determining whether older workers remained in the labor force" (466), but now, with employment pools that shift across countries, "continued employment is beyond either individual or local control" (466). In addition, our roles don't necessarily fit into these neat compartments any longer, and some of us may take on roles that others of us don't. Scholars such as Ferraro suggest that research that focuses on role transitions together with life trajectories "encompass[es] the rich diversity of possible outcomes and [seeks] to identify antecedents to them in the biography, historical time, and social resources of the individual" (315). What this approach allows, according to Ferraro, is the possibility of considering the "endogeneity of role transitions;" some "role transitions might include entry or reentry into the labor force, seeking or accepting a promotion at one's place of employment, or modifying domestic occupation because of child launching, remarriage, or custodial grandparenting" (319). Clearly, this list of possible role transitions doesn't apply to everyone; thus the need to check for them when conducting research.

SHAPING LIFE COURSES
TO EASE MORTALITY CONCERNS

To speak of aging, to speak of life courses is to raise issues of mortality. Authors such as Zigmunt Bauman argue that we shape our cultures so that our lives can have meaning despite the ever-present tangle of making sense of our own impending deaths. Our art, our cultural artifacts, remain after our deaths, a way of maintaining some immortality. This desire to leave something that marks our time on this earth helps individuals to navigate the complicated territory of death, something about which we may prefer not to speak. Aging is somehow always about our individual answers to what we expect from life. If we expect, in our fifties and sixties, to be experts contributing our best work, then to call oneself a basic writer, or an old fart, is to mark out the territory of fears—that what we know will no longer be as valued. The kinds of legacies we would like to contribute are endangered; those gestures towards something that might last longer than our own mortality are threatened.

Jenny Hockey and Allison James argue that the culture tries to avoid death by a series of slips and disguises. Sayings such as "young at heart" or that "old heads are said to be on young shoulders"; that "very elderly people may be described as entering a second childhood or as going 'gaga'" result in two consequences: first, the sayings "[suggest] similarities between the life experiences of very elderly people and children" and "secondly, it makes the elderly into metaphoric children" (73). Children in this culture are marked as dependent, so such a link marks elders as dependent. Hockey and James suggest that we disguise "the interdependence of people in everyday life" and create ways of thinking that "maintain dependence and independence as binary oppositions" (9). By associating elders with children, by linking their dependent categories through family metaphors, we "create distances and make distinctions between the worlds of adulthood and old age." Although "'growing up' leads inevitably to the time for 'growing old', the downward spiral," "through the metaphoric restructuring of time" by associating old age with childhood, "the wheel turns and death is seemingly subverted." From Hockey and James' perspective, then, "the concepts of ageing and disability should therefore be regarded as social constructions" (33) shaped by the culture to subvert the destabilizing threat of death.

COMBINING ALL THE FACTORS

To study aging and the life course requires attention to multiple variables. On the one hand, it seems fairly reasonable to assume that one could design questions that help to understand the individual's life course trajectory and how the individual fits within the larger societal structure, but on the other hand, such investigations direct us to the difficult territory of aging and potential societal strategies for coping with mortality. These concerns are not easily untangled. In our families, in our cultural frameworks, we shape a sense of identity based on gender, class, race, religious affiliation, region, body ability, orientation, and we bring all of our strategies, all of our entitlements (or lack thereof) with us when we approach this identity category that has potential to be discriminatory. Age gathers meaning through these multiple identities shaped by cultural, historical, and industrial traditions (Blaikie). Untangling identities is impossible, but gathering a sense of how each individual defines aging may be necessary for the research, depending on the goals.

Age, other identity categories, cohort experiences, and one's life course possibilities intertwine. If I need to decide on participants, does chronological and generational age matter more than cohort training in the field? How much should a person's ways of articulating identity count? How much should we consider life course expectations? Can we predict, in the case of Jane and my brother, which of the two will be open to learning new technologically rich literacies? We may not know what additional or unique roles either has taken on. Is one of them currently involved in custodial grandparenting? What kinds of issues should we check for when we create our research designs and how do we want to raise such topics and issues? In my existing research, I rely on chronological age as the initial screening criterion; however, I try to widen the range of ages and then ask questions that help me to gain a sense of the individual's aging experience, but I'm not sure I've examined the issues deeply enough.

Hagestad and Dannefer support "life-course analysis" that has demonstrated "the power of social conditions and social change to shape the outlooks, health, choices, and activities of developing individuals" (9), but they contend that the challenge in analysis is to somehow avoid getting by "'cheap,' testing the force of the environment by measuring single dimensions of a complex, multileveled environment (i.e., the cohort effect), and assuming that whatever variation is not accounted for by that test can be attributed to intraindividual processes" (9). A "bigger story" exists, "one linking proximal social contexts to more distal, macro level factors" (10). The challenge, for these researchers, is to somehow address these macro levels in combination with the individual actions while keeping a realistic sense of the possibility of agency.

3

NOT OLD FARTS

ERASING STEREOTYPES OF OLDER
FACULTY LEARNING NEW LITERACIES

> One certainty of technologically based knowledge is that the complexity of the instrumental aspects of learning tends to disenfranchise those who are not facile. Another is that as knowledge-based economies mature, those who represent previous ways of doing or knowing are depreciated in the eyes of those trained in the new technologies. Finally, though technologies in and of themselves are not solutions, neither are they problems. It is the meaning attached to them that creates disparities. (Cutler and Hendricks 463)

Recently, I was describing stereotyping research to an older friend of mine who looked at me for a bit and then said, "Angela, that sounds deadly dull." Laughing, I tried again. "Okay, tell me about two older adults who you really admire (and why)." We ended up talking about their positive traits, using terms similar to the research on positive stereotypes of older adults: astute, creative, enlightened, insightful, wise, trustworthy, fun-loving, curious, well-informed, sociable (Levy, Hausdorff, Hencke, and Wei; Hummert et al.). The list continued to expand as we talked. After a while, I said that according to some of this research, from the priming we've just done, your body has changed for the better. Because of our conversation's focus on positive stereotypes, your heart rate is probably different, your blood pressure and your skin have improved (Levy, Hausdorff, Hencke, and Wei). However, if we had discussed older people who make you worry about old age, you likely would have had negative physical responses. These researchers believe they can "prime" a person with stereotypes that influence physiological conditions, discovering the power of stereotypes on what we think of as automated bodily functions. These studies may have significant implications for my friend when she enters a workshop. If she evokes negative images of her aging self, those images may affect her learning. Can we shape positive images in these settings that might influence learning?

To arrive at positive images, more familiar terrain may help—the work of metaphor, the impact of metaphor on our imaginations. Margaret Morganroth Gullette argues that the narrative emphasis often found in aging research focuses on decline and mourning losses, and in an article linking her experiences of fashion with aging, she implicitly questions the ideological framework. She marks the stages or cycles of a fashion trend as similar to how we imagine aging within the field of aging studies, a similarity that could extend to how we think of literacy arcs. Following the life of a fashion product, she argues the following: "the known life of an object moves from purchase, through consumption (public display of possession), to the 'decline' (going out of fashion) necessary to start up the cycle again" and exclaims that the "metaphor that privileges the beginning" is called "the youth part of the cycle." "Youth!," she writes, "again yanking this chain of signifiers out into cleaner air, we find decline ideology" (35). As she describes her shopping experiences, the process of buying, wearing, and discarding clothes, she slowly builds this argument, comparing aging and decline stories to the discarding of outdated fashions: "we disavow the past in whatever mode we relinquish the prior object. It's not that the past is shameful, it is we who incur shame if we ally ourselves with the past, the unwanted, the 'old.'" (49). Further, she links this life course perspective to the larger market: "It is essential to the market system that we be constructed, by consumerism, to live the cycle even though the cycle implicitly devalues our sense of prior selfhood. Into the foreseeable future, then, people will go on learning to downgrade old knowledge, dispraise past objects of affection, discard them, and identify the renewed self with newly accepted values that despise the old" (49).

Her description gives me pause in terms of how we think about ourselves as we age and also how we think about "new" literacies. One could argue that this book is shaped by a desire to "help" people discard old knowledge, to acquire the newest fashions, conducting research that effectively gives us clues on the best practices for accumulation. If we are older, if we value aged literacies; if we are resistant to these new technologies, research could ease the pain of acquisition and ceremonies could assist in the discarding of "old knowledge." I want to believe that the text is not a transparent collusion in shallow goals and find some comfort in Nancy Kaplan's article on ideology, but inevitably, this tension exists. In conversation with myself, I justify/rationalize any potential threats of occupying such a position by convincing myself that newer literacies may be used to bring different populations to the academic conversations, but who decides which literacies are the aging ones, the inappropriate ones? How do I navigate histories that make it feasible for others to enjoy literacies I experience as laced with other kinds of exclusions (Maso, Selfe). If one feels pressured to discard that which has always brought pleasure, has helped one to shape a sense of identity, if one is supposed to be shamed into such an action, how comfortable am I? Inevitably in this thought process, I land in the uneasy realizations about commodification and our participations in structures that are never purely what we would desire. From that uncomfortable position, I worry over Gullette's critique, consider changing this book's title, and think about the dilemmas for all of us, when considering new literacies—ones that may mirror or parallel a culture fixated on youth and novelty.

If we adopt these metaphors, (of the fashion cycle, for example) if we live by them, we may unconsciously adopt attitudes towards those who are resistant to new technological innovations, the innovations that shape our definitions of literacies necessary for writing teachers. In addition, if we feel ourselves growing older, moving from the category of youth to middle or old age, perhaps we may begin to worry over whether our bodies will betray us, will make us appear "sick and incompetent" (a category of stereotyping Hummert et al. describe "Stereotypes" 243). We may try to change our bodies' external signs of aging, buying into the value of youth. How we and others read our bodies may cause us to turn to solutions offered by the dominant culture—we may start trying to modify our outward appearances, hoping this can keep negative assessments at bay.

YOUTH-CENTERED DENIAL STRATEGIES

One of western culture's ways of dealing with old age has been to bring it into alignment with the model of youth. In an attempt to "combat" the aging process, contemporary practices such as cosmetic surgery and hyper-fitness regimes in fact contribute to the cultural denial of aging through an artificial aestheticization of the body designed to approximate the depersonalized canons of youthful beauty. We need, individually and culturally, appropriate images of aging just as crucially as we need ways of mourning, ways of dealing with loss. (Cristofovici 270)

That we live in a culture that values youth is a given (Biggs 75; Greenberg, Schimel and Mertens; Gullette; Hockey and James; Woodward, Introduction xvii). On TV or in the movies, the paucity of older adults is apparent (Montepare and Zebrowitz; Palmore; Sherman). Markson, focusing on the treatment of older women, argues that "negative stereotypes about middle and old age in women's lives" continue because there is a "persistent belief that a woman's essence lies in her youthfulness—itself a symbol of her potential to procreate" (63). Although older women have more challenges than older men (Browne; Cruikshank; Hockey and James; Kaufman and Elder; Markson; Moen; O'Rand; Palmore; Rife 100; Woodward 87), both navigate a culture that values youth.

The images of elderly that we see are often of two types, according to Mike Featherstone. On the one hand "the 'heroes of aging' adopt a positive attitude towards the aging process and seem to remain 'forever youthful' in their work habits, bodily posture, facial expressions and general demeanor," and on the other hand are "those individuals who experience severe bodily decline through disabling illness to the extent that the outer body is seen as misrepresenting and imprisoning the inner self" (227). Featherstone and Hepworth assert that those who keep "their youthful beauty" are "the subject of praise," whereas those who don't are "seen to have failed" (29). The individual has responsibility to shape a youthful body. The dominant culture instructs us on the ideal we should value, and as Anca Cristofovici suggests above, asks us to construct ideas of old age by bringing ourselves in "alignment with the model of youth." Our way of making sense of our own aging is often to internalize this split "between a younger self and another self" (269). The outside self, then, becomes one that, through consumption of goods and products, can be manipulated to counter "the ravages which time has wrought" (Featherstone 223). In such a consumer culture, interventions on the aging physical body are the strategy through (Biggs; Blaikie; Featherstone & Hepworth; Hockey and James 76; Katz 69; Sawchuck).

Simon Biggs describes our culture as having a "preoccupation with novelty, childhood and youth culture," and it is a culture that needs a "deeper understanding of adult ageing" (2). A deeper understanding would require thinking against our ways of seeing aging as decline (Gullette 215). Shifting metaphors is intensive labor because our assumptions about aging are threaded throughout our daily lives. In casual conversations we make remarks that indicate just how thorough-going these values are. A professor calls himself an old fart, or Margaret Cruikshank points to our rationalizations for work that "keeps us young" (14), or young at heart, or we buy that adage that you're only as old as you think you are. All these everyday remarks reveal underlying assumptions, remarks, but we also need to pay careful attention to the particular contexts in which these stereotypes emerge, given the images we may be trying to escape of the "prototype *elderly person*" as "slow, confused, bent, and dowdy" (Cuddy and Fiske 10).

We may be trained by our culture to think of age in ways similar to old and new fashion trends, we may adopt certain body manipulations that would keep us "youthful" and therefore of value, and we may bring those values to the workplace, creating difficult situations in which to work and learn. These problems require an awareness of how stereotyping works and the unconscious treatment that results from these assessments of older people. Much happens on an implicit level when we assess and then treat people according to our sense of what they need (Braithwaite; Kite and Smith Wagner). Researchers argue that we often decide to use mental categories in order to streamline cognitive functioning: "to make sense of the world, we group objects and events based on their similar features" as a means of limiting confusion and overload (Cuddy and Fiske 4-5). In addition, Cuddy and Fiske would suggest that "at the root of stereotyping is our impulse to assign objects, events, and people to meaningful classes, about which we have established beliefs and expectations" (4). The problem comes when the stereotyping does not accurately reflect the situation or when, as Greenberg, Schimel and Mertens suggest, stereotypes of older people might in fact be a way of distancing: "In addition to physical distancing, people may also use psychological distancing to minimize the threat of the elderly" by calling them derogatory terms such as *"old fart, geezer, old-timer, blue-hair, codger, old hag, fossil,* or *dinosaur"* (38).

Stereotyping has powerful conscious and unconscious results. For example, we may unconsciously adjust our timing in interactions with others, accommodating our perceptions of the other's needs from pace in language to level of vocabulary. Even our gait can shift. Researchers have investigated the pace of walking in work on stereotypes of older adults. As indicated above, Levy and Banaji think that "it is possible that when young people are around older people, they adjust their behaviors in ways that reflect age stereotypes and thus activate the age stereotypes in older individuals" (62), and to support this position, they point to Bargh, Chen and Burrow's study in which they used "scrambled sentences containing words intended to activate age stereotypes. Although the priming did not occur subliminally, "the researchers found that participants in the stereotype group walked slower afterward than did the participants who had been in the neutral group" (62). This research is similar to the language-based focus of work with older adults and young students and their communication shifts (Kemper).

Mary Lee Hummert and her colleagues argue that stereotypes of older adults can be used to assess (correctly or incorrectly) a person's competence at understanding communication and that we adjust our speech patterns to accommodate our target audience. Stereotypes of older adults are not all negative, and in various studies Hummert has built on and developed categories into which elderly are often grouped. Like Featherstone, Hummert's research suggests a positive and a negative set of categories for older adults. In research in which young (starting at 18), middle-aged (starting at 35), and older adults (starting at 60) sort descriptions into categories, they found that all participants were able to create further categories within these two areas. On the negative side, they found that all participants established four categories for older adults: "shrew/curmudgeon" (ill tempered, complaining, etc), "recluse" (timid), "despondent" (hopeless, lonely), and "severely impaired" (senile, feeble). Younger adults added one more category: "vulnerable" (afraid, worried). Middle-aged participants and older adults clarified "severely impaired" by dividing based on degree—mild and severe. They also added a category of people they termed "self-centered" (miserly, greedy), and the older adults added one additional category—"Elitists" (demanding, snobbish) (246). On the positive side, they found that all clumped together descriptions that are termed "golden agers" (lively, happy, volunteer, etc.), and "perfect grandparent" (loving, family oriented, kind, etc.). Young and middle-aged adults created a third category called "John Wayne conservative" (patriotic, conservative, emotional). Middle agers contributed a fourth category "liberal matriarch/patriarch" (liberal, mellow). Older adults had a total of five distinct groupings, adding "Activist (liberal, political) and Small-Town Neighbor (quiet, conservative, tough)" to their lists (245). As we age, according to this research, we can clarify and categorize individuals more concisely. Where a younger adult only sees three categories, "golden-agers, perfect grandmothers", and "John Wayne Conservatives", older adults clarify personality types more concisely, providing five distinct characterizations.

In addition, in some of Hummert's research she found that "young adults were most likely to choose older age ranges (75 and older) for persons fitting negative stereotypes, whereas they chose younger age ranges (55–69) for persons fitting positive stereotypes (117). Young participants had different reactions than older participants. "Elderly adults have more complex stereotype sets than do middle-aged and younger adults, and middle-aged adults have more complex stereotype sets than do young." Hummert claims that "as individuals negotiate the aging process, their perceptions of the nature of aging change as a result of their interactions and personal experience" (117–118).

Attitudes and stereotypes may lead to beliefs about what kind of communications are possible: "Judgments of the communication abilities of the targets differed according the nature of the stereotype they represented. Respondents of all ages judged the two positive targets as experiencing significantly fewer communication problems and having better communication skills than the negative ones" (122). Hummert's various studies contribute to the research that indicates that individuals accommodate the perceptions they make based on stereotypes. If our gait shifts, if on numerous levels we shift our interaction with another person based on stereotypes, it becomes overwhelming to think about the multiple levels at which we might be impacted by treatment based on stereotypes. Although it is certainly true that we might benefit from language or a pace that accommodates our needs, the problem with stereotypes is that one falls into a category, and little room exists for individual differences to emerge or be addressed appropriately. Careful attention to context can reveal troubling communication strategies. Hummert's research examines the connection between stereotypes, communication strategies individuals take up with older populations, and the context in which the interaction occurs. In other words, it's not just that one might see older adults based on positive or negative stereotypes, but the context in which one encounters an older adult shapes the interaction as well. For example, a "golden ager" might be treated differently in a community center than in a hospital. Hummert et al. found that "even an initial positive categorization can lead to patronizing messages when the context undermines the stereotype" ("Communication with Older Adults" 146). This research reminds me to pay attention to the stereotypes people hold and their relevance within contexts. For example, we may want to study treatment of older faculty in two different contexts, one in which the faculty is expert, one in which the potential exists for the faculty to be treated as a novice. If we find that training happens in situations that promote more patronizing speech, we would then be wise to shape faculty development that draws on faculty's existing expertise and more forcefully examine assumptions that exist in these interactions, because the workplace research reveals that often potentially discriminatory attitudes towards aging participants may exist.

WORKPLACE ATTITUDES

> It is also possible that when young people are around older people, they adjust their behaviors in ways that reflect age stereotypes and thus activate the age stereotypes in older individuals. (Levy and Banaji 62)

Levy and Banaji's assertion that we adjust behaviors based on age stereotypes and negative interactions has the potential to spiral. More stereotypical behavior results in adjustments based on assumptions about aging that then cause the older person to behave differently, and a spiraling decline may occur. Research indicates that "younger people rated older workers more harshly than they rated their younger counterparts in the area of potential for development, qualification for a physically demanding job, and overall job qualification" (Kite and Smith Wagner 141). Cuddy and Fiske suggest that our ways of ranking older adults as high on warmth and low on competence may have implications for the workplace: "Younger employees and applicants are generally rated more positively than older employees and applicants" and "older people are perceived as less competent in job performance-related tasks than in interpersonal ones" (11). McCann and Giles add that several workplace biases exist against older workers, that younger people may rate older people negatively despite evidence to the contrary (173). In addition to younger people's bias, the career clocks managers bring to the workplace may shape expectations of older workers. According to McCann and Giles, "supervisor's evaluations will likely be influenced by societal norms that dictate where in the organization each worker should be at his or her respective age" (173, describing Lawrence's research). In Braithwaite's discussion about job discrimination, based on her research, she concludes that "older job applicants should be as successful as younger applicants, providing they are armed with social attractiveness," but acknowledges that "social attractiveness is a far more complex phenomenon in the outside world" (than in the lab) and that social attractiveness "is likely to be lower in cases where older job applicants have been denied access to new technologies" and "they are not familiar with new ways of doing work" (328).

If societal norms dictate our expectations for one another based on age, how do we confront those assumptions/expectations and undermine them? At this stage, we don't know enough about how our bodies are read by colleagues, by students, and by those who supervise us, and we need more information about what kinds of assessments people are making about our work that may have the influence of age-based stereotypes. Our research should assess how we internalize stereotypes as we age and the interpretations others make about us as we age. Older faculty may have stereotypes foisted on them by younger coworkers or students. However, we also need to pay attention to the kinds of stereotypes about age that older faculty place on younger faculty. Because we don't know how enough about how either are perceived, research should gather a sense of an older faculty's self assessments, but also explore the relation between others' assessments and faculty's performances.

RESEARCH THAT SUGGESTS SOLUTIONS

That we live in a culture in which old age is not as valued as youth is a given. Our responses to this reality are multiple: we may internalize our phobias and seek interventions that are designed to slow down our aging bodies; we may judge older colleagues more harshly and distance ourselves so as to establish our younger locations; we may have stereotypes about older adults that cause us to interact with our older colleagues in ways that are detrimental, by sending messages about physical capabilities (slowing our gait or our speech). However, we may be able to combat these stereotypes and our responses.

Stereotyping has implications that may be unconscious. Identity categories are always tricky to work with, but aging is unique in ways that make it difficult to assess. Amy J. C. Cuddy and Susan T. Fiske contend that "In first encounters, age is one of the earliest characteristics we notice" (3) and although we "form opinions based on sex, race, and religion, among other categories . . . old age is one that most of us eventually join" (3). "Unlike other groupings," they claim, "stereotyping people based on their age . . . goes largely unchallenged" (3). Even though stereotyping goes unchallenged, one would think that we would imagine ourselves as entering the category. Or, in Kathleen Woodard's words:

> As younger women turn these very prejudices against women older than themselves, they will in effect be turning against their very future selves as older women. If it is true that older women are more vulnerable than older men to the stigma attached to age and thus suffer more from negative cultural stereotypes, what younger woman counts

among her ambitions to be a little old lady or a wicked old witch?
(Introduction xiii)

This movement from outside a group to inside the group is noted in
Greenberg, Schimel and Merten's discussions as well: "If the elderly are
viewed as an out-group" it is an out-group that "the nonelderly will some-
day join if they are lucky enough to survive that long" (28). The ambivalence about joining this group affects all of us.

As with many identity categories, we may adopt cultural values without much conscious thought, making it a challenge to think about the
implications of our assumptions. We may not ever extend the logic as far
as Woodward suggests—that we will be doomed to the negative images we
extend to others. In part, the challenge is to understand implicit ageism,
the focus of Becca R. Levy and Mahzarin R. Banaji's research. They argue
that "one of the most insidious aspects of ageism is that it can operate
without conscious awareness, control, or intention to harm" (50). Unlike
other identity categories, "social sanctions against expressions of negative
attitudes and beliefs about the elderly are almost completely absent" (50).
Although there is a "lack of strong, explicit hatred toward the elderly," they
suggest that there is "a wide acceptance of negative feelings and beliefs
about them" (50) and that "ageism, unlike racism, does not provoke
shame, necessitating a study of what kinds of prejudices are implicit within our beliefs. They use an Implicit Association Test in order to "explore
individual and group differences in unconscious attitudes, stereotyping,
and identity as they relate to age" (52). This test, available on-line
(www.yale.edu/implicit) shows one kind of strategy that might be used in
research to measure implicit stereotyping.

The summary of their and others' studies indicates that "older participants, like younger participants, tend to have negative implicit attitudes
toward the elderly and positive implicit attitudes toward the young."
Interestingly, "all groups tested to date—other than the aged—invariably
show more positive implicit attitudes toward their own group compared to
nongroup members" (55). In attempting to make sense of this data finding, Levy and Banaji argue that the data "may be understood in the context
of the psychologically permeable nature of the boundary between age
groups," but they also point out that "unlike other groups, older individuals
tend to identify implicitly with the category of young as strongly as did
young individuals" (56), and in another study "the higher the self-esteem
of elders the more they both implicitly preferred youth to old age and
implicitly identified as young rather than old" (56). Hummert et al. have
recently suggested that part of the reason for this misidentification may

have something to do with not accounting for general slowing in older adults taking the test, so this research finding needs to be seen with caution. Nonetheless, if we all age, we all move towards the identity category of "old," but if we don't follow typical trends for other identity categories in how we come to see our selves, what are the underlying recommendations we might give to faculty about images they might hold of themselves? If, in fact, elders with higher self-esteem identify as young, how do we create literacy teaching that might help older faculty to benefit from this kind of disidentification?

Susan Krauss Whitbourne and Joel R. Sneed's overview of stereotyping research indicates that we may be able to intervene with positive images of older adults. They draw on research that suggest there is a relationship between stereotype priming and the speed at which participants walked. Summarizing Hausdorff, Levy and Wei (The Power of Ageism), they describe a study in which positive stereotypes of older adults were embedded in the participant's sessions. These researchers "observed improvements in gait under positive priming which were independent of age, gender, health status, or psychosocial status, strongly suggesting, as Bargh and his colleagues had previously shown, that negative stereotypes of aging can alter what might otherwise be thought of as strictly a physiological function" (265). This kind of research extends to our mental capacities. The authors point to a study by Levy that showed that "positive primes increased memory performance and self-efficacy beliefs, and negative stereotype primes had a detrimental impact on memory performance and self-efficacy beliefs" (266). The research suggests the possibility that a correlation exists between the images we evoke (or are called up for us) and the performance we imagine possible—whether consciously or not.

To be old is to have a limited set of options available to one within this culture (Blaikie; Hockey and James). Although we might not consider ourselves old, we have little control over dominant cultural biases. If we fit within the paradigm of elderly or older, we may face difficulties that are not of our own making—another person's assumption about us may influence our experiences. Students may reveal age bias in their assessment of our performances on teacher evaluations (Cuddy and Fiske 12). We may score high on warmth, but lower on competence if these stereotypes of the larger culture are placed on us (10). If we look older than the average fifty year-old, we may face negative stereotypes that shape the behavioral modifications people make for us (Cuddy and Fiske 15, 18). Each of these changes threatens to affect our behaviors, challenging our desire and possibilities. The arc of our literate practice's fashion and the arc of our individual body move together, and the stereotypes others assign to us, the stereotypes we activate may evoke issues of mortality, may cause us to examine our life course decisions and to enter, somehow, the territory of mourning and loss.

NAVIGATING MORTALITY

> What terror management analysis suggests is that whatever we do to try to promote more accurate and positive attitudes and behaviors toward the elderly, we have to do so in a way that is cognizant of the role of the fear of death in attitudes and treatment of the elderly. With a more sober and realistic understanding of our own fears and reactions to the elderly, we may be better able to understand ageism as something we are all prone to but nevertheless can combat. (Greenberg, Schimel and Mertens 45)

Some scholars make sense of ageism by pointing to the ways that older adults remind us of our mortality (Greenberg, Schimel and Mertens) or the transience of youth (Cuddy and Fiske 16). From such a perspective, how we engage one another in the midst of age may reflect our own strategies for making sense of death. How does one make sense of the knowledge that one will die? As Greenberg et al. suggest, "to be aware that one exists as a material creature in the world with a future full of possible threats and with death as one's only certainty is, as the existential philosophers have made clear, a very heavy burden indeed" (32). They ask "if we are in fact driven to survive and programmed to react with fear and defense to threats to our survival, how do we deal with the knowledge that mortality is our only certainty" (32). This conundrum. As Anca Cristofovici indicates, "loss and mourning accompany the discourse of aging" (269), and in some ways, thinking about death leads us to assessments of our life courses. This work may help us to navigate our memories, our decisions, given the "acceptable narratives" (Rossiter 66) available to us at certain points in history, but it also can be difficult work, because we may or may not fit with the life course expectations we think we should meet. Simon Biggs argues that "being on time or out of time with the accepted structure became a criterion for subjective satisfaction and socially valued norms of conformity (89). To evoke mortality and our relations to mourning/celebrating our own life courses, is to navigate very complicated terrain, which has the potential to become full of fears, worries, and baggage from past decisions for some participants.

Fear of aging, according to Valerie Braithwaite, "can be conceptualized like any other threat to our well-being. We can allow the fear to grow and dominate our view of aging, we can deny its existence, or we can try to come to terms with it, lessening its power over us in the process" (323). She describes two different strategies, the first emphasizing control—"pursuing an active problem-solving approach to aging at all stages of life is likely to prove beneficial. Individuals can learn more about the aging process, adopt a healthier lifestyle to lower the risk of poor health, plan for retirement, and make provisions for care, should that be required" (323). The second approach moves away from control. Drawing on the writings of Antonovsky, she describes his shift from "personal control to management." He:

> conceptualizes demands, that is, life events and hassles, not as abnormal experiences but as part of the normal state of living. In other words, Antonovsky starts from the premise that the normal state of living for everyone is more chaotic than orderly and that adaptation is a continuous creative process that involves us in learning, critical thinking, and effort. For Antonovsky, the never-ending threats from the inner and outer environments create tension that we relieve through using our resistance resources: freedom to enter new social roles, modify existing norms, feel connected to others, and have a strong sense of meaning in life and a belief that life can be managed. (324)

In our thinking about faculty training and development, we would be well served to create hospitable spaces in which individuals feel like they are connected to others, that they have a "strong sense of meaning in life and a belief that life can be managed." Too often, our local training doesn't help individuals to feel connected to one another and sometimes the training can be overwhelming. If people feel pressured to learn new technologies, and cannot figure out the new literacies, they may well feel stressed and unsure about their careers—particularly if they are in the more marginal positions within our field.

From the position of feeling threatened, people may resort to conservative strategies when it might make more sense to take risks. In research involving judges, Greenberg et al. suggest that when we are reminded of our mortality, we become much more inclined to enforce our worldview. In a study by Rosenblatt et al., "municipal court judges fill out a series of questionnaires and then make a judgment on a hypothetical case in which they needed to set bond for an alleged prostitute" (35). Through random selection, half of the judges were given questionnaires in which "two questions about their own death" were embedded. The researchers thought that if they "made mortality salience high for judges, they should be extra motivated to bolster their worldview by treating an apparent violator of that worldview, an alleged prostitute, especially harshly" (35). They found that the judges who were "reminded of their own death set an average bond of $455," whereas the other judges "not reminded of their own death recommended an average bond of $50" (35).

If we enter these training sessions thinking that we must discard the literacies we value, and if we see that within a framework of aging, if we evoke our mortality, whether consciously or otherwise, the situation for shifting literacies becomes fraught. To the degree that the shifting literacies can be seen as staying within one's worldview, the situation could be positive. If one's worldview is threatened, the event takes on different significance. Although the research is intriguing, we clearly need to create our own studies that give us a better sense about how individuals see these literacy shifts, and perhaps we need to be aware of how much each of us sees these shifts as destabilizing our worldviews.

The information on stereotyping and aging is thought-provoking. Multiple issues may be at stake in any given situation in which faculty training exists. To begin with, the material taught may or may not evoke resistance from the faculty—dependent, to some degree, on the extent to which the new material is seen as marking existing literacies as "aging," or "old-fashioned." If participation requires a faculty member to consider the aging aspects of his or her life, that may play into his or her responses—this faculty member may fall back on his or her worldview assumptions. If her worldview includes an enthusiasm about learning but her worldview privileges alphabetic literacy, she may find the situation bewildering.

The research possibilities on stereotyping are rather extraordinary in their range. We have much to think about regarding aging as it affects the acquisition of new literacies, from stereotypes people hold, to the ages at which those stereotypes are attributed, to the life course expectations shaping expectations. In addition, research on positive priming may be useful for shaping learning situations, or for understanding why some situations work whereas others do not.

4

SHAPING
RESEARCH/HYBRIDITY?

As the late Glenda Laws argued in "understanding Ageism," in order to understand ageism as a set of social practices with the aging body as its target, we must avoid essentializing the aging body. The experience of growing older is, in other words, profoundly shaped by the meanings which are ascribed to aging. (Woodward "Introduction" xiii)

Multiple research venues are necessary to understand the relation between aging (ageism), teaching and the accumulation of new literacies. What kinds of research practices from other fields and from our own we are going to be willing to adopt? How does one discover implicit ageism? Do we like the methods other fields use? Trust them? Do they help us assess/interpret what happens between generations in our field? A faculty member sees herself as a basic writer, or himself as an old fart, and I wonder about the actual possibilities for learning. How do we shape research that gives us clues on how a faculty member might imagine differently? How do we assess the implicit stereotypes? How do we assess the connection between what a person imagines and what that person takes on as possible within her classroom? Research may help us understand more about how to create the environment in which faculty are able to take more risks that don't leave them or their students making stereotypical judgments.

NOT BASIC WRITERS:
LEARNERS OF NEW LITERACIES

The question of how to improve training and development fundamentally raises the question of how we perceive literacy—both for our students and for ourselves (and I have a suspicion that our expectations for ourselves are different than the patience we give our students). How we think about literacy then plays out in the rhetorical situation—in the case of locating ourselves as learners (audience) in the rhetorical situation, our beliefs are tied to the positions we take when learning. How others perceive us in that situation also reveals their beliefs about literacy training. Not only does a researcher need somehow to tap literacy beliefs, but he or she must also try to understand the connections between beliefs and actions. Take the example of April from Chapter One. When she said she felt like a basic writer, how do we interpret her framing? At the time, I wondered what it meant for a professor to align herself with the marginalized, in 1999, when most of these technologies are already familiar to computers and writing faculty. I guess I wondered why she was not more familiar with the changes in technology. A good five years after Lemke indicated the changes, this woman appears to be hearing this information for the first time, and I would argue that in 2005, more than ten years later, she would not be alone if she still felt that way. Someone like Lemke can say in 1994 that our definitions of literate acts are necessarily going to need to change, but the university is a conservative place, and the pace of change can be slow, depending on location. I'm always curious about change, about how a person, a department, a faculty adopt different practices. How does the average faculty member adopt different practices, and what does it signify to make those shifts?

To what degree can we assess the impact of individuals' ways of knowing (shaped by their identities) on their abilities to accumulate new literacies? In other words, how do we interpret the "basic writer" comment, that stereotyping response—how do we test and contribute research on learners that explores possible correlations between how one thinks about learning and the kinds of strategies about literacy that one takes on? Second, if we know an individual's identity categories and the imaginary that they evoke, how do we interpret the images they give us and check for a correlation between imagined and actual practice? Third, can we suggest other imaginaries? And if so, can we develop research designs that help us to create those imaginaries based on participant input?

CURRENT LITERATE PRACTICES

Many have argued that literate practices are designed to maintain the current status quo. Those who have the power may be reluctant to give up any territory. When we think of a person knowing how to do certain things with language—as a means of marking literacy—we may forget the multiple literate tests, many of which can be shifted and altered in order to keep people in and people out. The bar can always be raised, even when certain literate practices are unnecessary for participation. Literacy tests may be used as screening devices not necessary to tasks at hand (Street 139-40). Defining literacy to include on-line conferences may appear, to April, an arbitrary bar to raise, one designed to make her feel excluded. Even if I would assume that April is capable of learning this material, she may opt out, as other forces shape what people think of as possible. As Tom Fox has eloquently argued:

> If we tell ourselves and our students that they will achieve access if they master writing standards, we are obscuring and underestimating the powerful forces of racism, sexism, elitism, heterosexism that continue to operate despite the students' mastery of standards. We are denying the terror that comes from economic insecurity; we are obscuring the effect that brutal physical violence has on women students; we are minimizing the debilitating effects of racial violence. (43)

What we can imagine, in other words, is concretely shaped by the realities of identity construction on lived experience (as explored by Mortensen, Stuckey, Taylor) and although Shannon would have us pay close attention to the issues of poverty and our ideologies (and critiques Stuckey and Taylor accordingly), we understand the literacy complications that are based on orientation, race, class, gender, or religious affiliation because members of our community have taken the time to explain how devastating the consequences can be for those who fall outside the normative gaze. Agency, in the midst of these bleak statements, is difficult. Nonetheless, for many literacy theorists, the goal is to widen the frame of the community, a more inclusive "conversation" with more voices at the table.

When a woman who appears to be middle-aged, white, and middle-class, full of the privilege of success within her chosen profession, leans over and theatrically says, "Why do I feel like a basic writer?" we may have multiple reactions based on our own assumptions about identity. "Hardly the same," we might say. "You can never know, really understand, the terror of that which is inaccessible." Or something equally as judgmental/condemning. But we don't know. We don't know how the individual shapes his or her sense of self in the midst of cultural pressures connected to identity categorizations. We may evoke an imaginary that reveals our ways of making sense of our identity categories, shaping a sense of self, a sense of what is possible in the midst of cultural pressures/expectations about how we are to behave.

Carol Dweck and Drucilla Cornell's writings have helped me think about how to design research that listens for the stories a person tells, the imaginaries revealed/refracted in those stories, and the strategies people employ to learn new literacies. Dweck's work suggests we might study already existing research on how children learn, as motivation may significantly affect our learning. Research on motivation would argue that the way we think about shifting literacies matters. What if we assume that we cannot learn what younger generations of writers know? Growing up with different media access, pointing to cable channels such as MTV or video games, teachers might believe that certain ways of knowing become hardwired into a brain, and those who don't have those experiences can never compete. Aging, in other words, may be articulated in such positions, marking out our cohort and what is possible based on what we experienced thus far. But such a position would best be checked with research. In John Hayes's article on literacy, he describes research that indicates a correlation between how we think of our relations to writing and the actual production of text. In other words, looking at people marked as basic writers, he suggests that one's self-perception may affect one's abilities to write. Those who believe that someone has a "natural" talent have a different response to writing, a response that may limit them. Discussing research conducted by Dweck, Hayes summarizes her findings:

> Dweck compared students who believed that successful performance depended on innate and unchangeable intelligence with those who believed that successful performance depended on acquirable skills. She found that these two groups of students responded very differently to failure. The first group tended to hide failure and to avoid those situations in which failure was experienced. In contrast, the second group responded to failure by asking for help and by working harder. One can imagine that if students believe that writing is a gift and experience failure, they might well form a long-term negative disposition to avoid writing. (181)

Dweck describes two kinds of goal motivation: (1) performance goals and (2) learning goals: performance-driven goals are ones in which one fears being seen as having "low ability." "If the goal is to obtain a favorable judgment of ability" children may not risk that which might bring "negative evaluation" (1041). In contrast, learning goals erase this evaluation component: "Children are willing to risk displays of ignorance in order to acquire skills and knowledge." "Instead of calculating their exact ability level and how it will be judged, they can think more about the value of the skill to be developed" (1042). Failures, when in the performance goal mindset, are evidence of a "lack of ability" (1042) whereas failures or "obstacles" in a learning goal mindset are seen "as a cue to increase their effort" (1042). The research is quite stunning, but has even more potential implications for women in English studies charged with learning something that alters what we know. Dweck overviews research on girls and boys, marking disparities between high-intelligence-scoring girls and boys. Bright girls are less likely to develop learning goals, more likely to play into performance goals: "Bright girls compared to bright boys (and compared to less bright girls) seem to display shakier expectancies, lower preference for novel or challenging tasks, more frequent failure attributions to lack of ability, and more frequent debilitation in the face of failure or confusion" (1044). Dweck suggests that these experiences/ways of seeing then shape areas of study—a bright girl might be more inclined to study English:

> New units and courses in mathematics, particularly after the grade school years, tend to involve new skills, new concepts, or even entirely new conceptual frameworks (for example, algebra, geometry, calculus). These new skills and concepts are not only different from but are often more difficult than those the children has mastered in the past. In the verbal areas, however, once the basic skills of reading and writing are mastered, one does not as typically encounter leaps to qualitatively different tasks, tasks requiring mastery of completely unfamiliar verbal skills. Increments in difficulty appear to be more gradual, and new units or courses often simply ask the student to bring existing skills to bear on new material. (1044)

In the case of computers and writing, of shifting literacies in the midst of technological change, I listen to people's often unnoticed beliefs about computers and generations. Some clearly think that only the younger generations can navigate new technologies. They are "hard wired," a sentiment that may be at the level of innate and unchangeable intelligence. If we believe this hard wiring happens through an extraordinary number of repetitions that we can't hope to replicate, it takes on an "innate" quality. Significant implications emerge for writing instruction, but more importantly, the stance needs to be examined. Does such a position then create a similar set of results to those of Dweck? If we think that learning this material requires mastery of something new—not building on verbal knowledge, will we opt out? What are the implications for intergenerational collaborations? Given our initial and continuing ways of imagining the threats/promises of accumulating various literacies, what necessary moves must be made to shift the aesthetics away from imaginaries that dominate and push us to assume ourselves out of the loop, to aesthetic images that create the opportunity to maintain a contributing voice (away from and in the midst of the stereotypes we [and others] create of our identity categories). At this juncture, we don't know enough about how writing faculty think. We don't know enough about how transferable findings are: that is, we don't know if presumptions about who can learn these changing literacies shape actual acquisition success.

The imaginary one evokes can reveal (though also always refract) much about what the individual imagines as possible. Clearly, the image of a basic writer is from only one person; others would evoke a multitude of images if asked. Nonetheless, I liked the frame because it fits succinctly with the kinds of responses I often hear regarding faculty training and development workshops in which the training fails—faculty feel that they aren't given enough time, that they can't understand, they have a sense of being out of the loop. They tell stories about missing steps that seem obvious in retrospect and about feeling silly, judging themselves harshly. Certainly not all faculty training and development workshops function this way, but when faculty aren't happy, their combined complaints often add up to the frustration that they are feeling like/treated like "basic writers,"[1] echoing a performance evaluation. Although research is necessary to prove that this is a collective experience, I know individual experiences enough to recognize this "basic writer" feeling as a useful image in considering the shape of research.

Why do I feel like a basic writer? This rich, complicated, and troubled image has at least two potential interpretations. As Bruce Horner and Min-Zhan Lu have summarized, when speaking of basic writers traditionally, the following dichotomies between "regular students" and basic writers have been used: "literate versus illiterate, college material versus remedial,

---

[1]Cindy Selfe and her colleagues at Michigan Tech try to avoid having participants in their summer workshops feel stupid or dumb (C & W 2002), a feeling similar, I would argue, to what this basic writer image evokes for some.

skilled versus unskilled, intellectually deserving versus undeserving." Frequently, the inclusion of basic writers has given rise to accusations of "diluted standards." Although the composition scholar may not have intended such an alignment (illiterate, remedial, unskilled, undeserving, and diluting standards), the choice of imaginary domains evokes these traditions and other traditions of race and class as well. Horner gives a history of CUNY basic writing and argues that there, "two types of students [were] set in opposition to one another: the open admissions students associated with politics and minority activism, and the ideal college students, assumed to be interested in and capable of pursuing academic excellence because they were not distracted by political interests" (8). That basic writing is associated with minorities and elides the presence of the white working class participants is a given.

That the current movement underway at many universities is a fazing out of basic writing is also a given. Open admissions appear increasingly a thing of the past. So the imaginary has within it identifications, if only momentary, with a tradition of race/class markings and unmarkings and decreased institutional support for particular populations. But the allusion to basic writers also has within it histories of enculturation and education. Mike Rose's *Lives on the Boundary* tells the stories of working-class students who were rewarded for rote memorization and the ability to do skill and drill routines while in high school. That preparation fails them when they attempt college because the requirements for learning and thinking are different. College not only calls into question earlier paradigms of formal education, but if we are working class and outside the mythical norm, we may have other paradigms learned in our families that are threatened and undermined by the ways of thinking valued in the academy. To be a basic writer is to mark oneself as Other, raced, classed, enculturated in ways not valued by the mainstream academic machine. So why that imaginary? Certainly such an association evokes an image of bodies no longer valued by academe—if basic writer's bodies ever were. To teach writing without the necessary literacies, to feel one's area of expertise as likely to slip away, might evoke one's allegiance with populations that seem to be in similar locations and may suggest stereotypes about aging as well.

The other interpretation possibility, however, is to see April as in a position of power, evoking the imagined basic writer as a savvy move, designed, whether consciously or not, to critique the means of conveying information. Grigar and company gave an excellent presentation, but it was lost on this particular participant. In the context of what we all know about basic writing, to evoke such an image could also be a significant critique. We are all familiar in the field with problems associated with labeling individuals as basic writers, and we don't want people to feel like basic writers—to be marked as excluded from the dominant academic games. But such a move, I would argue, places the onerous task of translation on the shoulders of Grigar and company. In such a move, if we assume a critique, the ignorance remains, but it's no longer the "basic writer's" problem. Eve Sedgwick said it well when she wrote:

> Knowledge is not itself power although it's a magnetic field of power, ignorance and opacity collude or compete with knowledge in mobilizing the flows of energy, desire, goods, meanings, persons. If Monsieur Mitterrand knows English but Mr. Reagan lacks, as he did lack French, it is the urbane Monsieur Mitterrand who must negotiate in an acquired tongue, the ignorant Mr. Reagan who may dilate in his native one.

Examining the image of basic writer gives these two possibilities for interpretation—at a minimum. As literacies shift we see savvy strategies for limiting change, some of which are more subtle and sophisticated than others. Raising up the image of a basic writer, given the field's worry over inclusion and exclusion, seems quite smart if the intention is to limit the possibility for change.

If, in fact, the move to basic writer was a defensive position of resistance, I have to admire the decision at the same time that it frustrates me. Although I have given April's comment, I'm using it because I don't know April at all, only in the broadest strokes—a vague familiarity with her areas of interest and a sense of where she plays in the field. From such a point of ignorance, I'm able to speculate more freely. I can well imagine a researcher who has risen in her field, who works extensively within her area of expertise—say assessment—who spends her research time gathering data, reading relevant materials in the field, shaping her courses based on her findings, contributing articles that help us to navigate assessment differently. She uses computers to communicate with others across the nation, to compile research data, to write her texts, but the thought of taking precious time away from her research in order to acquire knowledge about web pages, about courseware, about digital videos and multimedia text, may seem fruitless and pointless. How does any of this fit with her values? And as they cover all the possibilities and discuss challenges of architecture, her eyes glaze over. Little in the conversation is familiar enough to her own work for her to make the connections. What better image than the basic writer? It not only captures her sense of feeling lost, but it also critiques this foolishness.

When I imagine that April fundamentally believes this is foolishness, I want to know how much of her response is related to her sense of a life course and a career trajectory. I think of a friend who isn't too particularly keen on increasing her literacies regarding technology (at the same time that she often tries what others would resist absolutely—she takes on bulletin boards and course ware, web pages and instant messaging, etc.). My friend would say that she took up computers when first she saw them because she understood that they would facilitate what she already did— work with words. However, these shifting literacies move her away from the work with words that she sees as the challenge of writing instruction. These programs don't facilitate her work with words. Or rather, she adopts the programs that increase her possibilities for words—instant messaging—for example, but when the programs require more work than they seem worth—web pages—she isn't as interested. And I wonder, with both my friend and April, if they see themselves as at a point in their careers where they shouldn't have to change fundamental assumptions about words. Do their life course expectations shape what they imagine possible for their living? The life course imaginary we invoke for ourselves must play a role in how we hear calls for new literacies. If I have a certain set of expectations for life course trajectories, I might well be frustrated by a scene in which my knowledge is not praised and affirmed. The foreign feel might threaten fundamental life course beliefs.

The basic writer imaginary may evoke our sympathy or our ire for the means the person uses to navigate shifting literacy demands. To develop the best practices for faculty curriculum, however, the basic writer comment needs to be assessed so that we can create training that neither excludes the audience members nor places the onerous task of "knowing" on those who are in the role of teachers. When we place a teacher in the role of one presumed to know, and student in the basic writer position, we've created a troublesome situation. Research should figure a way to help us move outside these tangles.

In Drucilla Cornell's *At the Heart of Freedom: Feminism, Sex, and Equality* she emphasizes the necessity of allowing each individual equal opportunity to "share in life's glories" (32), but points out the complications that occur when one group's sense of life's glories are imposed on another group. Cornell is primarily concerned with our "sexuate" beings, and the necessity of clearing the necessary imaginary space, and perhaps connecting her agenda to this text may seem a stretch, but to some degree the connection holds: Like Cornell, I want to explore how the imaginary shapes the kinds of spaces we create and to suggest spaces that enable more of us to participate. The curious issue at stake in the basic writer image is whose

imaginary is imposed upon. The issue of groups and their power is implicitly a part of the discourse communities in which we participate.[2]

For my purposes, the question of faculty training and development is
important to this imaginary domain because how we learn, what we can
learn, matters to our ability to accumulate necessary literacies, the literacies
that help us to "share in life's glories." Although Virginia Woolf and subsequent generations would question the degree to which one could share in
life's glories while within the structure of the university, and although the
ideal state would somehow, for me, include a utopian socialist reality in
which learning wouldn't necessarily be tied to economic capital, and economic capital would not be necessary to live out life's glories, this fantasy
has not yet worked its way into reality. In the meantime, I want to suggest
that participating in the current academic structure needs to begin with an
awareness of the complexities of continuing to share in life's glories as we
move through our life cycles, as the literacy requirements increase, and as
we attempt to accumulate the literacies that come to matter.

Cornell defines the space an "imaginary domain" which "is the space
of the 'as if' in which we imagine who we might be if we made ourselves
our own end and claimed ourselves as our own person" (8), a place where
we can "create an ideal representative" of ourselves, perhaps, but not necessarily marked by the dominant conceptions of us. To evoke the basic
writer as "an ideal representative" of herself is certainly this professor's
right, particularly if this technology learning has within it the sense of an
imposition by a dominant group, but what other images—what ideal rep-
resentatives might also be feasible? What work might we do to reimagine
the university and our role within it, given these issues of technological
advancement, aging literacies, and the possible threats to our senses of
selves. How might we work productively to shift and correct, to reimagine
and create in the midst of what we know about literacy and aging, in the
midst of what we know about writing and our relations to alphabet literacies, among our many other literate practices?

---

[2]I want to also make this a "woman thing." As Cornell argues "elite men have long
been given the right of self-representation" whereas women "have for too long
been judged capable only of passive imagination and the ability to mimic the persona deemed proper for women" (11). I want to suggest that the call to see one's
self as a basic writer is a repetition of a larger imaginative space, marked out by the
dominant and elite. Our participation in the university, as women, only happening
in significant numbers within the last thirty years, our participation edgy at best,
means that the image of a basic writer might well suit our sense of things, but we
should be conscious of the ways imaginaries we evoke repeat the "family systems"
at work in the university.

Literacy work has traditionally paid attention to the stories people tell, listening for what they believe to be possible, looking for patterns that might mark behavior as revealing a sense of race, class and gender, and so forth. Literacy work pays attention to the individual, attempting to understand the relation between the dominant cultural beliefs and the internalization of those beliefs by the individual. Scholars have explored the ways that writers compose, from a variety of locations, reminding readers of the complications in communication that occur because of identity expectations marked on the body by the cultural inscriptions (Brodkey, Cushman, DiPardo, Dunn, Farr, Gilyard, Hawisher, Heath and Kirsch, Malinowitz, Mortensen, Selfe, Smitherman, Sullivan, Villaneuva [to name only a few of multitudes of texts]). What we imagine possible, what we believe to be obstacles, may have much to do with cultural inscriptions about race, class, gender, orientation, regional affiliation, body ability, religious affiliation, adopted kinship practices, and age. Cultures define what bodies can and cannot do by setting the terms of engagement based often on identity categories. Who can marry, who can have access to government resources and at what ages, who can speak and in what venues are all governed. Because we are, to some degree, shaping our imaginaries based on our identity categories and our interactions with the dominant culture, it makes sense to examine the narratives/roles we choose. This is particularly important as we all will face challenges with technology. Although I think current literacies are accessible, I cannot imagine what will happen in the next twenty years. If my personal life affects my decisions about "keeping up" with technology, I hesitate to think about what it might feel like to be in the position of catching up with people who teach but have little patience for my newbie questions.

In our conversations about literacy, we have acknowledged the role that the body plays. It shapes our sense of what kinds of exchanges can happen (Butler). Society plays a profound role in shaping a body—the expectations, the access, the availability all contribute to dominant perspectives on who can and cannot participate in our multiple communities. We know well enough how we come to imagine what is possible, the ways that we come to participate willingly or unwillingly in our classified/assigned roles. People who have attempted to change their location with regards to the dominant culture's values on literacy describe the high cost of shifting categories. Working-class academics, for example, speak eloquently to the challenges that occur when trying to enter locations not accessible (see for example Ryan and Sackrey, *Strangers in Paradise*). The gaffes occur because literacy enforcement happens not only in texts but in the ways a person negotiates in meetings, the timing of humor at parties, the casual conversations in hallways, what we reveal, what we conceal. Class lessons, learned from childhood, shape our sense of how interactions should proceed. Many in our field have addressed the ways in which the movement into the categories reserved for the mythical norm has been challenging and the devastating consequences of trying to fit.

When we think about the possibilities of literacy eradicating discrimination, we often end up arguing that acquiring the necessary written literacy practices does not adequately address the complexity of literate interactions. Simply knowing about different behaviors doesn't necessarily translate into possibilities because our bodies are part of the exchange. Although my own experiences have always been positive concerning computers, many have negative experiences with computers that shape their ways of negotiating new technologically rich literacies. Thus I understand the complexity of suggesting simply that people adopt different images, or "as if" situations, that might ease literacy acquisition. However, experiences could perhaps be shifted by multiple repetitions in which alternative images are put forward. I am not suggesting that if we just shift the images, we will automatically be included in what are always already exclusionary domains. However, Dweck's description of children may support a different mindset: "Retraining children's attributions for failure (teaching them to attribute their failures to effort or strategy instead of ability) has been shown to produce sizeable changes in persistence in the face of failure" (1046).

Part of my research includes exploring alternate imaginary domains, given the power of positive and negative priming discussed in Chapter Three. As a scholar in composition studies who often reads in cognitive psychology, and two years ago studied on a grant with the National Institute of Aging, I often think of myself as a tourist, or as a consumer at a flea market. Each of the images allows me particular attitudes. Reading about research projects completely outside my enculturations, I often feel like I am a tourist, taking snapshots. Or I think of my friend who is an artist in mixed media and plans her weekends around flea markets, looking for material that will shape her work. When I'm reading statistically thick material, trying to get my head around foreign concepts, instead of feeling like a novice, an apprentice, or a basic writer, I instead imagine a role that affords me some status. As a tourist, an "artist" (of sorts) at a flea market, I have more space for my authority. Familiar with what matters in my field, I sift through information, looking for finds. The tourist persona allows me to maintain a sense of expertise; it also eliminates the thought of others as potentially judging me (performance goal) and shifts to an emphasis on learning. Although the images aren't ideal, I offer what I imagine to suggest the possibility of finding other imaginaries because I believe that what we imagine profoundly influences our ability to participate (Dweck), and also because we need to examine the imaginaries we have and the possible implications of certain ways of seeing.

The problem with this suggestion is that the imagination is shaped by our relation to the communities in which we work. Acquiring a new way of thinking about material is never actually as easy as it would seem because we all participate in the exclusion and inclusion of others based on our culturally informed/enforced expectations of what people can (or will be allowed to) accomplish (performance goals). With aging particularly, we need to examine our own stereotyping tendencies, recognize the points of culturally informed/enforced expectations, and counter debilitating images, ones that detract from participation. We need to think and imagine differently. A woman in her mid-fifties, stands in a room in a conference, leans over, says dramatically, "Why do I feel like a basic writer?" And I think, well, what are her options? What kind of image would make sense for us to hold up as we move towards increasing pressures to acquire technological literacy? Many images are possible. We could see ourselves as musicians in a small jazz group. Or we could imagine ourselves in roles that are perhaps more familiar to us as writing teachers—as a group of colleagues who contribute to a center, or to an interdisciplinary major. What I want to imagine is some sort of collective group that moves away from the audience role of "basic writers" and the rhetor role of "all-knowing teacher" to a more collaborative and fluid relation, one that assumes that if we keep the current dichotomies, we will never actually reach the potential we already have in our community. If my friends and colleagues would take up these literacies, they would provide insights because of their expertise. Their years of experience matter. It is a complicated negotiation, often full of intergenerational territorial struggles/issues, but if I thought of it as a gathering of musicians who came to play on a Saturday afternoon, in a downtown Kansas City bar, the imaginary evoked allows for different collaborations than the imaginary of a basic writer and a teacher who is failing the basic writer.

The group of musicians is but one imaginary; the interdisciplinary department or center is another. In other work, I've argued that we need to address some of the accumulations of literacy by thinking outside the frame of "individuals," to rethink university structure/design so that we can give people more time than the frame allowed by the university's current semester structure. Those are grandiose goals, though not outside the scope of the possible—just more complicated to achieve. We need to think of a collective that works on technology acquisition together, that we afford collaborations to keep up with the many shifting technologies. Although we might have the goal of a collective group all sharing similar literacies, it doesn't seem that feasible to imagine we can all do all things. Instead, we could imagine a classroom differently, with various participants contributing different literacies.

When the focus is on aging in the discussion of literacy accumulation, what we might find are significant and revealing assumptions that tell us more about identity construction than perhaps we would like, but also indicate why understanding identity still matters. If I invoke an imaginary that fails to establish agency, how can I hope to participate? When shaping research on faculty development and training, I'm curious about the stereotypes that people evoke when they describe their reactions to a workshop or an overview of technologically rich literacies and their possibilities. One of the difficulties is figuring out ways to hear the imaginaries invoked and to understand potential reasons for different imaginaries.

The complication in listening to the stories participants in research tell rests precisely in the difficulty of understanding the statements made. As the basic writer example shows, several interpretations fit, not the least of which are the strategies faculty employ in order to escape the frame of outsider and maintain influence over which literacies will matter where. Some professors may seem to crave a time gone by, and we should cautiously approach these issues of literacy to allow for the amazing talent that one finds in new literacies and to allow for the traditional kinds of literacies valued in the academy. If we respect both kinds of literacies, we should be careful not to reinscribe literacies that have kept people out.[3] This chapter raises questions about how we can shape research that enables a discussion of the stereotypes/imaginaries invoked and also aid a group of participants in coming up with a collaborative imaginary that might work for them.

In this project, I have repeatedly asked myself how to shape research to come up with such solutions. Instead of an audience of basic writers and a teacher who fails the basic writers, we need research that gives us more clues on how to train, clues that might move us out of the polarities of trainers and learners, keeping in mind our desires, worries, and frustrations with this never-ending push to acquire new literacies. Such research may gain from looking at psychologists' work with motivation and from further contextualizing of the problems for the predominant population of writing teachers: women.

---

[3]For a debate that clarifies these kinds of positions, see the Selfe/Atkins conversation in JAC.

5

GENDER AND AGING

CUMULATIVE (DIS)ADVANTAGES

Women's and men's roles and resources are *socially constructed*, a consequence of the different life paths and stereotypes that exist in our society. These factors can contribute to a lifetime of cumulative advantage for men and a lifetime of cumulative disadvantage for women. (Moen 189)

A *cumulative advantage-cumulative hardship pattern* [occurs] in which lower initial levels of most or all forms of life-course capital interact and are compounded over time to place minority groups, and especially African Americans, at permanent and perhaps increasing disadvantage relative to others with age. The second is a *deflection pattern*, or a developmental sequence in which the significant infusion (or depletion) of some form of life-course capital redirects the economic, social, health, and/or personal trajectory away from initial circumstances. (O'Rand 204)

I have been thinking of my next career, of late. My grandmothers have lived long lives; if I follow their traditions, I need to plan for sixty more years. As a result, career counseling sounds sexy right now. In the book store, I pick up the texts that help readers select future employment. My students tell me about their dream jobs, and I imagine myself in their shoes. I'm browsing now, though I have about fifteen years to decide. Some days risk sounds appealing. Shouldn't a Crow know how to fly? Or maybe direct air traffic? Other times, artsy directions seduce. What about architecture? I floated that idea by a friend of mine the other day who said, "Be careful. That profession has the highest suicide rate—all those creative people doomed to draw boring designs." Sigh. Stuck in front of a TV procrastinating, I watch detectives on my favorite show, or Judges, or other social police jobs, thinking, they're not all that different from teachers. Not such a stretch. But maybe I want a stretch instead? Although plenty of time exists in which to make a decision—twenty years at least—I've taken to interviewing others. Visiting my brother, I found myself asking his kids what they wanted to do when they're older. Maybe they think I'm interested in their futures; I'm really fishing for ideas. I'll wager that this second career will require retraining, perhaps more graduate work. The thought isn't overwhelming, because some of my colleagues have done it. With first careers that were in other industries or in their homes, in their forties or fifties, these women returned to graduate school, earned Ph.Ds, and began tenure track jobs in their midfifties. Not a bad idea, considering the life span of the average Crow. Although my quest is somewhat leisurely, and without a lot of financial pressure attached to it, I know that for some women, the decision to return to school was driven by a need to earn money. If a woman has divorced after raising children, she may not be able to live in conditions comparable to those she had while married without working. In addition, choosing (unpaid) care-taking careers affects the time at which she can retire.

If a woman works in the home, raising children or attending to an elder family member, our economic structure does not recognize that work by counting it towards social security. Nonetheless, women continue to provide the majority of elder and child care (Browne; Carp; Cruikshank; Hockey and James: Richardson; Moen; Scott; Settersten and Lovegreen; Woodward.). At younger ages, a woman is more likely than a man to quit a job to raise children and have a career trajectory marked by discontinuity (Markson 63). At older ages, more frequently than her male siblings, she provides care for her parents or her spouse's parents (Carp, Moen; Scott). This unpaid labor traditionally seen as women's work, these expectations, "these responsibilities strongly condition women's educational attainment and enrollment and their attachment to the labor market" (509). This conditioning leads women to decisions that have consequences for old age. A woman may give up her outside career in order to do family caretaking work: "Employed women who become caregivers in late midlife are more likely to retire from their jobs" (Dentinger and Clarkberg, cited in Moen 180). In addition, women experience tension when their families expect them to give care to grandchildren or elders (for example, see Facio 339).

If the conditioning is strong, one would assume that resisting the expected role will be costly at an emotional level, in part perhaps because "the centrality of the family is drawn upon to make manageable the notion of human need" (Hockey and James 126). Unpaid care-taking labor supports the current societal structures of inequity (Hockey and James 145). Cruikshank estimates the value of "women caregivers" paid at a minimum wage to be "87 billion" annually (citing Wood 122). As Browne maintains, "the functionality of assigning women to caregiving is recognized as being beneficial and cost-efficient to society" (131).

Women's lives, according to Moen, "are typically *contingent* lives, shaped around the experiences of others" (189), and Moen interprets these "choices" women make as socially determined: "Women's and men's roles and resources are *socially constructed*, a consequence of the different life paths and stereotypes that exist in our society" (189). O'Rand argues that underlying the life course is "the latent construct of stratification or inequality as a fundamental and pervasive, but complex, social condition" (197). That inequality, she contends, is held in place with "economic, social, and psychosocial components" and operates at multiple levels "across societal planes extending from the economy and the state through the community and household to the individual" (197) and "is not fixed, but dynamic in its effects on lives over time" (197). Scott similarly points out that "rather than viewing the family as a social sphere where different norms operate and women play a major complementary role vis-à-vis the work sphere, families are viewed as operating according to the same kinds of power agendas as the social structure in which they are embedded" (369). The family is the traditional location, Scott argues, for the "early sex-role socialization and devaluation of women" (369).

In qualitative research with Suellynn Duffey on aging and faculty training, we noted the similarities among the four women participants. These women were involved in child care throughout their lives, and during our study (one academic year), two of the women were caregivers for an elder parent, a third participant was taking care of her granddaughter who had come to live with her, and the fourth had a daughter at home. In shaping research, I haven't often thought to ask questions about grandchildren care or elder care, but if we're to understand the realities our faculty face, we need to consider caregiving and other financial pressures because training situations may tax a limited amount of energy and we need to know what other constraints might be infringing on a person's abilities. We also need to ask difficult questions about affect—what if the proposed literacies aren't interesting to the person, what if that person wants to conserve her energy, giving her time to other concerns?

When we examine the potential impact of aging on a group of writing faculty gathered for a workshop, we might think, ah well, we're involved in the challenge of understanding various ideas about aging and stereotyping challenges, but we should pay attention to how age intertwines with other identity categories. Thirty years ago, Susan Sontag argued that women faced double jeopardy with aging because they were discriminated against for being women and then additionally for being old. Along those lines, an older female person of color may face triple jeopardy. Although theorists argue about the degree to which double jeopardy exists (see, for example, Susan R. Sherman), aging research does pay attention to and theorize about the interrelations of larger institutional structures and individuals' experiences within those systems based on gender, race, and class. Protocol questions should assess women's issues because writing faculty are more often women, particularly in the position of adjunct. Although we know figures from MLA on part-time and full-time labor (Lawrence), and who teaches composition (predominantly full-time non-tenure track, part-time, and graduate student TAs), they don't segment out gender and race in their study. Nonetheless, one can both draw from existing research (Enos; Miller) and local examples to see the disparity of women to men. At my own institution, 70 percent of the teachers of writing are female, 30 percent are male. As almost all of our faculty are full time, and as everyone teaches introductory composition courses, these percentages reflect a range of writing teachers from tenure track to temporary positions. At one of my alma maters, among the adjunct and TA labor the percentages are similar—69 percent female and 31 percent male. The percentages are significant to a discussion about the training and development of writing faculty. Part of the workshop structure must not only include paying attention to the gaps that can establish a relationship of those presumed to know and those who are seeking knowledge, but leaders should also attempt to understand how strategies are shaped by multiple identity concerns. Untangling age, gender, race, orientation, region, religious affiliation, body ability and so forth is a daunting task. Nonetheless, one can start to see some patterns.

With multiple identity categories, cumulative advantages and disadvantages may emerge. The images of women are often more derogatory than those associated with men (Biggs 75; Greenberg, Schimel and Mertens; Gullette; Hockey and James; Woodward, Introduction xvii), and these derogatory images may contribute to perceptions about women who are perceived of as old before men are (Kaufman and Elder; Rife; Sherman), though how much of a gap in age differences is up for debate (Sherman, with the most conservative number, marks the disparity at about 5 years. 22). Similarly, if one compares older adults based on class or race one sees apparent disparities. Authors argue that these differences may lead to a cumulative advantage or disadvantage (Ferraro; Hockey and James; Markson; Moen; O'Rand; Palmore; Williams and Wilson). Margaret Cruikshank gives the following example:

> The long-term consequences of class difference can be illustrated by simple examples. A middle-class professional woman in her twenties can afford to buy an IRA each year, but the woman her age who cleans her office cannot. Forty-five years later, the former may have accumulated several hundred thousand dollars, the latter nothing. To acquire this wealth, all the first woman has to do is to keep breathing. Very likely, her husband has a secure job that, like hers, will provide a pension. Their childcare expenses take a smaller percentage of their salary than of the office cleaner's wage. Moreover, the working-class woman's parents will probably need her caregiving help sooner than the parents of the middle-class woman. If the working-class woman and her husband manage to save enough for a down payment on a house, they may be denied a mortgage because of redlining, a form of discrimination that will never impede the upward mobility of the middle class couple. (116-117)

Although we may take issue with some of Cruikshank's renditions of the situation, the scenario makes the point—we can see the disparity that emerges and accumulates over a lifetime. As people of color and of lower classes are at a "cumulative disadvantage" according to these writers, the risks faced are higher, particularly because of the consequences of poverty on health. However, Cruikshank's example is of a certain kind of middle-class woman, someone who works 45 years at steady employment. Many middle-class women do not (for discussions of class identity, see Jones; Wright). One has only to ask writing teachers to list out their places of employment, to chronicle their entrances and exits from the workforce to see the disruption of labor due to (grand)child or elder care.

POVERTY

According to Williams and Wilson, "across all racial groups, women are more likely than men to be poor" (165). In fact, "although women constituted 58% of the total elderly population, they are 74% of the elderly poor

(165). Rife provides additional information: "In old age women of every marital status have lower money incomes than their male counterparts due to lower wages, inadequate pension coverage, economic dependency on men, and widowhood. The median income for all women 65 and over remains only 56% of that of old men" (93). Virginia Richardson indicates that "in contrast to retired men, many retired women experience marked reductions in income following retirement, and they often lack pension coverage" (54). Colette Brown suggests that "conservative policies fail to uncover relationships among poverty, discrimination, and poor health. It blames women for their poor health, and fails to see their lives from a life-span perspective" (131).

This poverty is linked to work patterns. Again, according to Browne, for middle-class women who did work, "more often than not it was in part-time, segregated and low-paid employment, and with years taken off for family caregiving duties" (167). To contrast, "divorced and minority older women—whose work histories are more similar to White men's, at least in number of years worked—find that discrimination, segregated employment, and lack of access to private pensions have dire ramifications for their economic survival" (169). For divorced and minority women, Browne points to the cumulative consequences of "restricted educational opportunities, limited educational attainment, no credit in Social Security or pensions for the years spent caregiving, segregated employment, and jobs that pay lower wages due to not only segregated employment but discrimination" (129). The life-span experiences indicate that the "economic well-being of women is threatened more greatly than that of men by life events such as divorce or separation, death of the spouse, birth of a child, loss of proximity to other family members, disability, or loss of work due to illness" (Carp 113).

At first glance, we might not link writing faculty to these statistics. However, many part-time adjunct faculty may actually subsist at or below the poverty level, and research on writing faculty should somehow assess this issue (see Nelson; Lawrence; and Schell and Stock). Understanding poverty and older women is important to the population of writing faculty because stakes may be high when it comes to training and literacy accumulation. In addition, middle-aged faculty may be taking care of mothers who would fall within the category of poor, with few resources for that care taking. If we took my brother Greg again, my friend Jane, and Jolene, a temporary instructor as examples, we might see this point more clearly. When Greg reaches 58, is ready to retire and is challenged to learn new technologically rich literacies, he may see it as entertainment. Having always enjoyed learning, he may come in ready to play with no real pressures, and as all of his kids are raised, and as his sister is charged with elder care for their aging parents, he may have all the time he needs to practice what he learns. Jane, at the start of career (57) may worry that she won't catch on quickly enough, and because she is involved in both child and elder care, may face significant time challenges. Jolene may have the most at stake: she's 60, has had health problems, worries about how she will pay for insurance if she loses this job, and is sharing elder care with her sister. Location matters—and the challenge is to somehow figure a way to learning that helps faculty grasp material in the midst of different realities.

HEALTH

The consequences of poverty and the working and living conditions of lower class experiences for men and women, are played out on the body. The cumulative argument that works for other disadvantaged identity categories functions here as well: "Most or all forms of life-course capital interact and are compounded over time to place minority groups, and especially African Americans, at permanent and perhaps increasing disadvantage relative to others with age" (204). In addition to economic capital, Williams and Wilson indicate that "noneconomic forms of discrimination may also adversely affect the health of the African American elderly. 60% report that they have experienced chronic, everyday experiences of discrimination" (170). The consequences of this difference in income is marked on the physical health of individuals' bodies, with "women of color . . . disproportionally affected by many diseases" (Conway-Turner 119). Not only do people suffer from more stress-related health problems (O'Rand 204), but with the "weaker national welfare institutions" (206), "growing economic and social inequities within populations yield negative outcomes in health and well-being" (197). The bottom line is that "disadvantaged groups still live shorter lives with more years spent in poor health than their more advantaged counterparts" (199). Not only does poverty contribute to poor health but discrimination affects the treatment people receive. Margaret Cruikshank reveals that "minority elders" are "underrepresented in clinical trials" on drugs tested, and that "at every income level, black women over fifty-four are only half as likely as white women to have a mammogram ordered" by their health care providers (97).

In the study that Suellynn Duffey and I conducted, two of the most tenuously positioned writing faculty had significant health concerns. As I think about the issues at stake in accumulating literacies, I am always cognizant of how these worries accumulate. If I'm on medication that challenges my ability to pay attention, if I'm tired from taking care of a grandchild, if I wonder whether my contract will be renewed, what role do these factors play in my ability to learn? I have yet to be involved with writing faculty where there weren't these kinds of worries. Those in the position of marginal instructors often have much at stake, and we need to understand the pressures writing teachers face.

LIFE-COURSE MODELS REVISITED

O'Rand's statement, that underlying the life course is "the latent construct of stratification or inequality as a fundamental and pervasive, but complex, social condition" (197), can help to understand the disproportionate fall of women into poverty. Whereas the traditional life-course trajectory follows a tripartite of education, work and retirement, "women's life paths are neither orderly nor neatly segmented, as they move in and out of education, employment, community, and family roles" (Moen 183). In the typical model, males are the focus and the "developmental model is simply applied to women (the nonstandard case). Then 'women's problems' are noted as exceptions to the standard" (Sinnot 149). Sinnot argues that "we are not doing a good enough job in capturing the richness and complexity in the development of mature women" as a result of not having adequate models (149).

As Cutler and Hendricks suggest, "women and minorities may have a hard time identifying with the concept of a career trajectory when their work histories were anything but stable, orderly, or progressive. But the notion of career-like trajectories came to dominate conceptualizations of adulthood" (466-67) A focus on class, gender, race, and age reveals the heterogeneity of life courses. Cutler and Hendricks would attribute this heterogeneity "in terms of well-being and status" to be a "reflection of society-wide patterns over the course of their lives" (474), patterns that establish who is able to "control, exchange, and retain goods and resources, including food, weapons, money, property, or knowledge" (Markson 55). Moen points to research by Settersten and Hagestadt that marks "few clear deadlines for family or occupational transitions (181) and Henretta highlights the "increasing heterogeneity in the pattern of individual work careers and retirement pathways" (255). Some of the theorists might connect this heterogeneity to the radical changes in civil rights and women's rights of the late 1960s, whereas others would point to the shifting market economies that function at a global scale. Given the inability of the local economy to control access to jobs, Cutler and Hendricks propose that "the notion of career tracks may also need to be modified, as a succession of entry-level or noncumulative positions becomes typical" (467).

The notion of heterogeneity of the life course is an important one. In my own experiences of interacting with women in the academy, I increasingly note the impact of making different choices in terms of life-course options. In the first years that I taught at Georgia Southern, I tried to categorize the women who had earned Ph.D.s in Composition and Rhetoric and had taken tenure-track positions at our university. We were split pretty evenly in terms of age (three in the thirties, three in the fifties/sixties); most of us had pursued Ph.D.s within a fifteen year period. All of the six women had been married/partnered and divorced. The older women had returned to school after children. The three women who were married/partnered again were with these men who were "wifely" in my experience of them; the woman's career seemed (to me to be) the dominant one. Three of us were single. Our experiences were different from the women who had taught longer in our department, who were predominantly from the area and had often earned their Masters degrees at Georgia Southern.

The three older women had chosen caretaking (sometimes as their primary responsibilities) initially in their life courses whereas the three of us in our thirties had a different kind of life-course agenda, aligning more with trajectories conventionally held for men, though with significant differences. None of us in our thirties had children, though one of us was involved in elder care. None of the six of us fit with the paradigm familiar to most of the others within the department. As I try to make sense of how to shape research to address these life course differences, the challenge is not only in attempting to understand a woman's partner's role in her life (i.e., is the partner the one to take care of family concerns? to give up career pursuits?) but also to understand how we perceive each other, given the choices we've made

We may not see how our life choices fit within larger cultural/cohort patterns. We might characterize ourselves as having made choices on later marriages, "fewer children . . . later in life"; and we may see ourselves as less "financially secure [than] our parents were in their middle age" (Ray 117), but we wouldn't necessarily see that as a pattern of baby boomers unless we read these characterizations and recognized ourselves as making similar choices. According to Tomlinson-Keasy and Gomel, "90% of married women" remained at home with their "preschool children" in 1950

whereas in 1988, 50 percent of women with these age children were working (346). Women who were adults in the "late 1960s and early 1970s . . .
faced new ideas about women's roles . . . as well as new opportunities to
pursue occupational careers of their own" (Vandewater and Steward 375).
In that time frame women experienced "changes in attitudes regarding
women's roles in the labor force, greater access to equality in higher education, use of birth control, greater acceptance of divorce, and renegotia-
tion of roles within the family" (Scott 367). According to Moen, "for the
birth cohort of women born between 1955 and 1959, fewer than half will
be in first marriages by age 50. Indeed, nearly a fifth of this baby-boom
cohort will be divorced" (374). Although we know to be careful about giving broad generalizations about a cohort's lived experience (Ray 119), such
information can sometimes remind us of the significant similarities within
a cohort and the significant differences between cohorts.

When we are thrown together in workplace environments, we must
navigate our disparate choices. Thinking about life courses means we
inevitably must examine our ways of knowing, our beliefs that are so thoroughly influenced by the cultures in which we are raised, by the ideologies
the state would have us uphold, by the values our family thought necessary
to enforce. Encountering each other, in the midst of our generations' experiences, we may or may not be pleased with what we see. Younger generations may "take things for granted" that older generations fought for. Locked
into certain expectations shaped by larger economic structures that depend
on inequities, locked into conceptual frameworks that value men more than
women, we may look at each other and be angry that we have not had the
same opportunities or made the same choices. In addition, the values of
one generation may seem to implicitly critique the other generation.

The difficulty is in the potential intergenerational conflict as both
Woodward and Ray eloquently point out. Woodward suggests a perspective
shift as a way out, reminding us that "there are more than two generations
of women in the academy" and that we are not limited to the frame of an
"Oedipal struggle" (89). The contexts from which we read the actions of
other generations matter. Speaking about Nancy Chodorow's interviews
with "women psychoanalysts who had trained in the 1920s, 1930s, and
1940s," Woodward writes: "We must remember to respect the differences
rooted in history. We have no right to expect to hear the answers we would
give to the questions we ask of generational others. It is a vain and imma-
ture enterprise to wish either to be mirrored at our age (what is it? How old
are you? *Tell*), or to enter automatically into struggle" (90). Similarly, Ray
explores the challenges of thinking about conflict that happens between
generations as more complicated than just Oedipal struggles. When we

navigate these literacy accumulations, we will do so within life course values we have adopted. Paying attention to the values we've chosen may help us to understand the role regret plays.

Given the generational and cohort influenced ways of knowing and learning, what methods or what strategies should we use in literacy accumulation? How can we be sensitive to women's different experiences with life-course trajectories? I think sometimes people may want to acquire new literacies if they see themselves as on a certain career trajectory that includes a correlation between technology thick literacies and a rise in prestige. However, an individual may find his or her worth from other locations, and the job is not central—is not where one shapes an identity. To ask people to devote more time to the job at the expense of family concerns may result in the loss of writing teachers. The consequences of these kinds of pressures are enormous and may play a role in writing teacher's dilemmas regarding the teaching of writing. In addition, even if these women want to learn, they may be faced with home situations that deplete their energies.

To some degree, in this kind of economy, those with the least resources may be forced to learn the kinds of technologically rich literacies that will ensure their ability to teach writing. To return to the example of April from the first chapter, we could argue that she enjoys a certain luxury. As a tenured professor, secure in her field, it may only be peer pressure that pushes her to accumulate literacies, and not the fear of job loss. These disparate positions needs to be understood. What are the effects of job security on learning? How comfortable will individuals be revealing what they don't understand about a concept? How does this learning experience fit with others? And always, at the back of some of the participants' minds may be this fear—if I cannot learn this material, what will happen to my job? I think we need to figure out how to conduct research that deals with what is internalized in these fears and how we might best navigate a global economy that shapes our sense of what we must learn.

Faculty come to training sessions with the identities that they've shaped over time. O'Rand cites Thoits, who suggests that "the accumulation of role identities (self-evaluations of efficacy and competence relative to cultural expectations) is the foundation of self-esteem, which in turn is found repeatedly to be positively correlated with psychological and physical health" (202). The information is intriguing. If we are asking older faculty to learn these new literacies, and they feel that their efficacy and competence are threatened, we may in fact contribute to psychological and physical ill health. In addition, the responses may reveal much about the navigation of earlier childhood experiences. But it's a difficult set of issues.

Take two participants: an older (57) white male, a full professor with comfortable job security, and an older (57) white female who is an assistant professor. Both come to the technology with some hesitations; both are from lower socioeconomic childhoods. The man shows some frustrations but keeps a positive attitude and takes risks. The woman is outwardly hostile and while she learns the material cautiously, one senses that she does so at great emotional cost. Can we make sense of these responses by pointing to class? To class and gender? Or to life trajectories and the male's ability to choose a certain life course? If we take the image of April, the person who feels like a basic writer, how do we untangle these identity categories? If we find out that she has a working-class background, do we attribute her remark to her class training? Or is her reaction more a mark of her gendered self?

Although we may not be able to link a response to an identity category, (i.e., she behaves this way because of negative internalized gendered/classed messages), protocol questions about race, class, and gender can lead to the discovery of patterns that might correlate to identity categories. An older black man who is a temporary professor reveals to the researchers that he has hypertension and that new medications require adjustments that he hadn't anticipated, that he feels drowsy most of the time. Or an older white female who is also a temporary professor indicates that the prescription costs associated with diabetes are too expensive, creating the necessity to take on more sections, and that although she'd like to afford a computer at home, she cannot, nor can she reliably count on the computer at work to be available. We may be able to draw on the research about gender, race, and class to interpret these comments, determining from protocol information what role caretaking or racial discrimination has played in career trajectories. Although we cannot easily tie actions to one identity category, the information available about older women, people of color, and information about class can help us to make sense of a person's current situation.

To return to my life plans for when I am sixty, I imagine the delight of learning. However, when imagining my future learning situation, I hesitate to be thoroughly enthusiastic, as I don't know how my body will age, whether arthritis or other conditions will impact my career choices. In addition, others' life decisions may shape my own; unanticipated care-taking may fall to me. Whereas current learning is tied to identity, perhaps at fifty–five or sixty, I will think I'm too old to learn new literacies, even with the promise of forty additional years. Or I may want more authority than a novice position allows. When we conduct research on aging and writing faculty, many factors compete for our attention. I imagine that our locations and choices as women shape our experiences. At almost forty, without kids, with choices that are afforded by not having taken certain caretaking roads, if I hold a workshop on Flash, I can imagine some of my colleagues muttering something about my lack of time constraints. But if someone who has caregiving responsibilities were to give the same workshop, the sense of possibility might be greater (i.e., if she can do this, so can I). We don't know how gendered expectations shape learning, but we should pay attention. The knowledge about race, class, and gender also needs to be tempered with information about what happens to our bodies as we age. All four aspects need to be considered together.

6

SENIOR FRIENDLY TEXTS?

INVITATIONS TO RELATION
AT THE TEXTUAL LEVEL

Recently, my friend's partner was convinced that something was wrong with her brain and had a battery of tests done. The doctors, shaking their heads, informed her that her scores were some of the highest they had seen. When I met up with the two of them at a conference, some conversation topic came up about her magnificent brain, and my friend's partner exclaimed, "You know, I used to be perfect." We laughed, but she was halfway serious. As a teacher of languages, she swore she never made errors. Now, from time to time, she'll make a mistake like the rest of us mere humans. Not wanting to alienate my friend's partner, I resisted the inclination to explain what we know about how our brains change with age. I've learned that it's okay to say I study aging, but to actually discuss what happens to aging bodies seems more taboo than bringing up feminist ideologies in a fundamentalist Sunday School class (having tried this too, I don't recommend it).

Given my experiences in day-to-day living with the responses others have to aging research, I am tempted to put a warning label on this chapter; to say, if you don't want to know some cursory information on aging and brains, eyes, and motor control, don't read this section. Curious, no? Why can't we talk about what happens to our bodies? Maybe Hockey and James's work will help here. They argue that we live in a culture absolutely bent on infantilizing children and older adults, and within dominant cultural spheres, independence and dependence are polarized (9), interdependency obscured. I understand the fear of being dependent and the way a discussion about body changes evokes worries regarding independence. Although my identity has never been based on about having the biggest brain, fundamentally, I shape identity in the act of learning. My intellectual abilities are one of the foundations of my sense of self. So for me to be dependent, to lean on someone else for intellectual help, is anathema.

Nonetheless, I'd rather know what is happening to my brain. I don't know why it doesn't bother me to study texts that tell me that the ability to read text changes as we age, that our working memories shrinks, or that eyes will shift. These changes are self-evident. I don't run as quickly as I used to (not that I ever ran quickly) and presume this general slowing is happening everywhere. Once, I could hold a thought through a student's tardy entrance, through whatever room repair noises, and so forth. Now I have more difficulty. Is that aging? Or is it merely the accumulation of students coming in late. (And is that another kind of aging?) The eye doctor informs me that my eyes are changing, which explains why it takes longer for my eyes to adjust to light and darkness (Echt 67; Mead, Lansom and Rogers 92). As I age, I want to enter situations where my specific needs are appropriately addressed. The design issues, the invitations to relation, must occur in such a way that participation remains a feasible option. This requires attention to room design and computer manuals, to handouts/manuals/on-line help material.

TEXT DESIGN

In the scenario that opened Chapter One, John instructs Mary on filter rules, establishing what I imagine is a gap in the exchange, a gap that may have much to do with creating readable instructions. Mary, over there on the side of frustration, says "help!" and the help provided may reinforce tired positions of the one presumed to know and the basic writer. Or so I think. When John suggests that Mary "learn how to use the filtering rules that are built into [her] mail program" and to "create rules that sort all messages with the subject text 'Out-of-office' into the wastebasket," I'm pretty sure he intends to give useful information, but I fear he has assumed Mary knows quite a bit more about computers than she does, an under-accommodation. I want him to get it just right, an extraordinary challenge.

Perhaps comparing two texts will help me to make my point. As I'm writing this morning, Anne Wysocki's text "Impossibly Distinct" lies on one side of the computer. In this text, Wysocki cogently articulates the differences in assumptions about audience, informing us that each time we create and design the architecture for information dispersal, we must, inevitably, assess the audience we invoke. Wysocki likes to be treated as a complicated thinking subject; this much is clear. The invitation she would most accept appreciates her mind, her skill and craft. She is not interested, at least for the genre she describes, in the creation of a simplistic definition of "accessible" design if such a definition means straightforward navigation. Wysocki's writing sits on one side. On the other side of the desk, "Making Your Web Site Senior Friendly: A Checklist" counters Wysocki's kind of invitation to relation. From the look and feel of the text, including its architectural structure, the emphasis assumes an audience who face many barriers. The requirements for "senior friendly" may not extend an adequately respectful invitation to relationship if one keeps Wysocki's values in mind.

These two texts' proximity reveals a problem: we do not know enough about how well older and younger adults negotiate the designs that Wysocki compares. What impact does one's expertise in the subject matter play? What role does one's educational background play? How does one's computer literacy shape the experience? What role does the assumed invitation to relation have? Can one make the somewhat rigid and simple suggestions for making a web site (or cd-based text) 'senior friendly" without speaking down to an audience? Well-designed text, shaped for a sophisticated audience, might be in tension with the recommendations given for senior-friendly site development. The problem speaks to us, as all texts do, about the complications of creating readable text. Faculty development and training happens in the midst of changing literacies. For example, with the advent of the web, we can see a shift from a reliance on alphabet literacy to multiple literacies, and writing teachers increasingly need to be able to teach in such contexts. However, shifting to on-line text may impact some teachers' abilities to read if they have vision trouble or mobility challenges (Echt; Worden et al.). In addition, we are multifarious in our experiences of aging. Some people experience "normal" aging whereas others encounter challenges that limit mobility. A fifty-five-year-old woman might have arthritis, for example, and experience difficulty maneuvering a mouse—something that affects her ability to read a web page with numerous small "button" links. Another fifty-five-year-old may experience minimal mobility challenges on-line. The aging process is experienced differently, and that diversity limits our ability to make predictions about older adults' physical and mental experiences when learning new ways of teaching writing.

FRAMING WYSOCKI

Towards the beginning of her article "Impossibly Distinct," Wysocki discusses various names that could be applied to the person who decides to view the information she is describing: "[W]hat to name the person in front of the computer screen? How to label the relationship between that person and what is on screen?" After reviewing possibilities, she says

> [A]ll these names are uneasy for me precisely because my considerations of multimedia pieces on computer screens indicate to me that some of what is at stake in how we approach the visual aspects of screens are the relationships—reflectively critical or (and?) pleasurably dependent or (and?) creatively participatory or (and?) . . .—we wish to establish with what is on the screen. Because how we name ourselves represents the relationship that we wish to or think we have or have inherited. (211)

Her questioning of the relationship we wish to establish (inherit) is precisely the issue with NIA's document design recommendations for older adults. In these discussions about web design and older adults, one must be seen as an older adult, the invitation to relationship requires this identity articulation. What if I don't want to be an "older reader?" If I think of myself as able to negotiate issues that they say I can't, how do I enter into the domain of "older reader?" If I'm writing for "an older reader," what exactly am I assuming about my audience?

In Wysocki's text we move through an argument that begins and gathers force as she makes her way through two interactive cds. Beginning with the openings, she describes the differences she sees between the two texts: "If the Barnes screen pushes out at me through the stern and large face of Doctor Barnes looking at me, this Maeght screen starts to pull me in" (214). From these introductions, she moves to the presentation of art: "The Barnes CD presents its art to me statically and from straight-ahead. The Maeght CD gives me multiple and moving perspectives" (218). In a section called "Differences of Scale, of Time + Space," she concludes that "unlike the Barnes CD, then, which gives me a quick, spatial visual structure for comprehending the whole collection, / the Maeght CD gives me a long temporal structure: I can only begin to comprehend the whole collection if I am patient, letting the video unfold" (219). As her comparison continues, we start to see what Wysocki values about the Maeght CD over the Barnes CD: "I feel respected by the Maeght CD in a way that I am not by the Barnes CD" (230).

> I have to think about why the CD has been arranged as it has; if I want to feel I have any sort of hold on the presentation, I have to make my own paths through it; they are not handed to me. Although the CD is not asking me to question my relationship to art—or to artists or to arts foundations—it is encouraging me to question how the arrangement of the CD contributes to my understanding of it . . . a first step in encouraging me to be aware of my interpretive part in moving through such a piece. On the other hand, the Barnes CD hands me everything. (230).

Wysocki acknowledges that "it is easy to be frustrated by having to figure out where you'll go when you click something, or by not easily finding your way back to a particular screen" and describes "discussions with others who received this CD as part of the software delivered with a new computer and who started to look at it and gave up quickly, unable to figure out its structure" (230). Nonetheless, the Maeght CD, from Wysocki's perspective, addresses her as "someone who is thoughtful and patient and intelligent enough to make the effort" (231). I like this focus on the kind of invitation to relation that is extended to the audience, and am challenged to think about how one accomplishes such an invitation, given the "senior-friendly" web site guides. I'm also amused: Wysocki's print text is organized in a traditional way, helping us to follow her argument. She would perhaps argue that the article's structure reflects an instance of the appropriate use of the straight forward organization, that art audiences are different, and perhaps this response would work for senior-friendly web sites as well.

SENIOR-FRIENDLY GUIDELINES

Wysocki describes the less ideal text: static, straight ahead, with a quick spatial visual structure. Navigation is easier and interpretive leaps are fewer. It assumes an audience member role that Wysocki rejects. Instead, she wants multiple and moving paths, long temporal structures, to make her own paths and to be challenged in navigation and in the interpretations she gathers from her movement through. Such a CD gives Wysocki a sense that she is addressed as a thoughtful, patient, intelligent "reader." Wysocki's perspective becomes intriguing when examining the following material from the National Institute of Aging (NIA), a senior-friendly guide full of recommendations for creating web sites for older adults. From the NIA's perspective, text that we create needs to be highly attentive to the physical and mental shifts that happen as we age. In what follows, I've chosen to simply provide lengthy excerpts from their information for two reasons: first, these are the guidelines that are being disseminated; second, they provide a succinct overview of information available in several interrelated fields of study. From their compendium, then, the following information:

Age-Related Reductions in Visual Function

There are reductions in specific visual functions with age that are important to consider when designing web-based materials. These include acuity, contrast sensitivity, visual field, eye movements, and the ability to discern colors (see Echt, 2002, from which this categorization is summarized, for a more in-depth discussion of this topic).

Acuity, or the ability to resolve fine details is the primary source of visual problems in older adults. Therefore, the size and arrangement of relevant text and graphic details are important considerations in screen design. Presbyopia affects how well materials can be seen close up and often makes small type sizes difficult to read. This condition can often be remedied with corrective lenses (Bennett and Eklund, 1983). Larger type sizes may also be used on a web site to circumvent this problem. The combination of reduced contrast, low luminance, and glare may further reduce acuity, even with corrective lenses, especially for persons over the age of 85.

Contrast sensitivity is the ability to discern luminance differences for targets of different sizes and is reduced with age. This means that older adults may need 2 to 3 times more contrast than younger adults in order to discern characters that comprise most text. Consequently, it may be necessary to increase the degree of contrast between the focal object and its background in screen design to mediate age-related changes in contrast sensitivity. Hiatt (1987) suggests that this can be accomplished by increasing the difference of the two on a gray scale by at least 2-3 values and also by careful use of color, texture and size variations (see Charness and Bosman 1992 for a more in-depth discussion on illumination, glare, and contrast sensitivity in printed materials).

Visual field or the ability to detect information from the periphery shows marked declines as one grows older. The result is that older adults are not able to detect the presence of text or graphics on the outer portions of a screen when focusing on the center of a screen. The implication of the reductions of visual field on screen design is that layouts should not be so complex (or contain so many elements) that they crowd equally important elements to the outer edges of the screen.

Eye movements are necessary to acquire information from the screen. Because of age-related changes in eye movements, older adults are likely to have difficulty reading from crowded screens or screens that contain too much information. Therefore, it is important to keep layouts clean and simple.

Finally, **the ability to discriminate colors** declines with age. This is especially true for violet, blue, green, and yellow ranges. Colors of the same hue or de-saturated colors such as pastels are also difficult to discriminate, as one grows older.

Reductions in certain visual functions that occur with increased age are characterized by a gradual onset (Verillo and Verillo, 1985). Normal age-related changes in vision do not occur suddenly. However, when all of these changes are taken together, they can affect one's efficiency in using information technology. The guidelines listed below for web site design are intended to make text more readable online and act to compensate, at least in part, for some age-related changes in visual function just described.

Motor Coordination

It is very possible that older adults will experience difficulties with fine motor coordination such as using a mouse when navigating through a web site. Riviere and Thakor (1996) demonstrated that older adults were less successful in performing a tracking task with a mouse than were younger adults. Older adults have also been shown to be slower and less accurate than younger adults when using a mouse (Walker, Millians, and Worden, 1996). In addition, they have more problems in clicking and especially, double-clicking (Morrell, Dailey, and Echt, 2000; Smith, Sharit, and Czja, 1999). Older adult's problems with mouse movements were found to be related to age differences in perceptual feedback, strategy, and increased error when applying force to a mouse (Walker, Philbin, and Fisk, 1997). Walker, et al., 1996 also observed that for the very small targets (3 pixels), older adults had difficulty hitting the target—their accuracy rate was 75% for this target compared to 90% for larger targets (6, 12, or 24 pixels).

Cognitive Aging

Working Memory: One of the clearest findings from basic cognitive aging research is that older adults perform less well than younger adults on a variety of verbal and spatial working memory tasks, especially as the tasks become more complex;

Text Comprehension: There is ample data from basic research in cognition and aging indicating that the ability to comprehend text also decreases as one ages;

Perceptual Speed: Perceptual speed is the speed at which mental operations are performed (Salthouse, 1993). Many studies on cognition and aging have reliably demonstrated that older adults are slower than younger adults when performing most types of cognitive tasks (see Craik and Salthouse, 2000). This finding has also been consistently documented in the performance of computer tasks (see Charness and Bosman 1992; Czaja, Sharit, Nair, and Rubert 1998, also see Morrell and Echt, 1996, 1997). Furthermore, older adults also may slow down their reading time to compensate for stress (Meyer et al., 1996). Thus, presentation speed is an important factor to consider when planning for optimal comprehension or recall of text.

Recommendations

Style
Present information in a clear and familiar way to reduce the number of inferences that must be made. Use positive statements.

Keep the text as simple as possible as researchers have found that older adults are less able to make inferences from recently presented information and are less able to disregard irrelevant information than are younger adults (Botwinick and Storandt 1974; Hoyer, Rebok, and Sved 1979).

Phrasing

Use the active voice.

Phrasing is important to increase the comprehensibility of a sentence. Most researchers agree that using the active rather than the passive voice is more understandable (Park, 1992).

Simplicity

Write the text in simple language. Provide an online glossary of technical terms.

Easy to understand vocabulary is beneficial for all users, but especially for older people. The use of technological jargon should be avoided because older adults may not have backgrounds in software or hardware terms. Subject areas such as law or medicine may have terms that are either unknown or confusing to the average reader. When the use of these terms cannot be avoided, provide a glossary that is easily accessible to the reader.

Organization

Organize the content in a standard format. Break lengthy documents into short sections.

If the web site offers a variety of information, clearly label each section so that users can quickly locate items of interest. Older adults perform better if they finish one task before starting another so organize the web page so that each item is displayed or discussed completely before presenting the next (see Park, 1992; Hartley 1994 for general discussions on how to present printed information to older adults).

Long documents

If a lengthy document is provided, break it into sections. This not only makes retrieval easier, but also assists the user with finding the information he or she wants without having to wait for the entire page to load (Morrow and Leirer, 1999). Avoid large, complex graphics because they increase download time (Nielson, 1997, 1999) and cannot always be interpreted by screen readers used by visually impaired web users (Mead et al., 2002). Provide a summary of long documents at top of page so users can quickly determine if this is the information they are looking for.

Navigation

The organization of the web site should be simple and straight-forward. Use explicit step-by-step navigation procedures whenever possible to ensure that people understand what follows next. Carefully label links.

Navigation is the path that users take to move around a web site as well as to link to other related sites. The larger the site is, the simpler it should be (see Rogers and Fisk, 2000). Web sites with many pages can be confusing if the navigational structure of the site is not clear. It is always important to provide an easy way to return to the home page.

Memory Cues

Label each page with the name of the site, preferably using the same design and location on every page. These visual cues provide environmental support to compensate for memory lapses (Morrow and Leirer, 1999).

Some of this information is self-explanatory, but other parts may need a bit more clarification, particularly the cognitive aging portion. Cognitive psychologists are curious about what happens to our ability to process information as we age and tend to focus on something they call "working memory" to explain how we function in seemingly simple tasks like reading the newspaper (Miyaki and Shah). I tend to accept perspectives that suggest we have a general working capacity for our working memories and that as we age, our working memory capacities shrink, affecting the speed and efficacy with which we can process material (Baddeley; Daneman and Tardif; Hartley; Just and Carpenter; Stine). Others think that we have decreased performances because of a general slowing in the body (see Salthouse; Burke's overview). We are 1.5 slower at many cognitive tasks at fifty compared to our twenty-year old selves. These theorists would argue that the speed affects the amount of material that is present for processing. We process more slowly, so we have declines in our performances.

Theories about working memory try to make sense of how we process information. As Shah and Miyake concede, "it is not easy to figure out what working memory really is" (1). Studies try to test various parts of models, but how working memory actually functions is still under investigation. However, the term *working memory* is a way of understanding what happens when we're faced with certain kinds of mental tasks. For example, right now, visual and audio information is informing me of my surroundings. As I type, I'm dividing my attention between the screen and the view from my window, watching college students as they go about their days. Music from one of my favorite cds plays while I try to remember facts and wring my hands, wondering if my favorite cognitive psychologist would roll her eyes at my ways of imagining working memory. A stack of quotations and a working memory paper from a course long ago help me as I create sentences, paragraphs, arguments.

I don't know what my working memory capacity is; however, if I don't jot down an extraneous issue that I need to cover later, by the time I get to "later," the point is forgotten. I think that means my capacity is not at genius level. In addition, as my working memory shrinks, I'm not sure how strategic I am in the use of my resources (Gernsbacher and Faust; Stine). Some theorists would argue that our working memory capacity just shrinks as we age, so we're not able to hold as much information as long; information just decays too quickly. This has an impact if one reads through a document in which important information on page one is significant to a decision necessary on page four. If the information has decayed from page one, the appropriate inferences won't be made (Kemper).

Theorists develop models for how that information is processed. For example, Baddeley and Logie conceive of a central executive area from which two components function, "a phonological loop and a visuo-spatial sketch pad" (29). The "central executive" monitors, "focusing and switching attention, and activating representations within long term memory" (28). My ability to write this text in the midst of all the sensory information and activations is the function working memory is accomplishing. Working memory theorists try to create studies that will reveal how we juggle multiple tasks at once, and they attempt to understand a crucial element for faculty curriculum design, namely, "how experts or skilled individuals maintain task-relevant information during the performance of familiar tasks" (Shah and Miyake 14). Working memory is a complicated concept, but the research from the area is of significance to us because the information shapes recommendations regarding readable text. One can see these kinds of recommendations in the above compendium. When they suggest that we create documents that reduce inferences, they're relying on certain findings about how we process information. They also have significant studies on how older adults hear sentences. Some sentence structures are easier to understand than others, similarly to the structures in overall documents. The population they study, however, is often much older than the dominant population of faculty.

The issue and challenge is how to take all of the recommendations regarding older adults on-line (Bikson and Bikson; Echt; Holt and Morrell;

Lamson; Mead and Rogers; Morrell and Echt; etc.) and make sense of them for a particular population. When cognitive research looks at older adults surfing the web, many of the studies are often too general. Can these guidelines be more thoroughly articulated so that we can gather a range of possibilities for older writing faculty? I want to believe that it's possible to imagine visually interesting text, text that invites an intelligent audience with these guidelines in place, but I don't think many of their suggestions are compatible with the extension to relation Wysocki imagines for audience. I try to imagine what she would do with the recommendations—how she would create visual/alphabet text that reduced inferences, simplified navigation, and still engaged the audience she imagines.

Susan Kemper has addressed this problem of how to create appropriate text for the audience with research on under and over-accommodation. When a text is perceived as "insulting and patronizing," we might describe that material as "over-accommodating" an individual. Employed with aging adults, over-accommodations "are often marked by the use of a special speech register, termed secondary baby talk or elderspeak" (30) which can have a negative spiral effect (see Ryan et al). To contrast, under-accommodation may "lead to comprehension failure" (Kemper 30) because the rhetor assumes the audience receiving the information understands more than the audience actually does. In the example presented between John and Mary, I would argue that John under-accommodates Mary's needs. Similarly, the Maeght CD may under-accommodate many viewers—as Wysocki states, there were other people who "started to look at it and gave up quickly, unable to figure out its structure" (230).

Kemper et al. have studied over- and under-accommodations in laboratory settings, asking older adults and younger adults to give each other directions to a location, using a map. In those studies, they discovered that "young adults will spontaneously adopt a form of elderspeak when paired with older adults"; they "use more utterances, directions, and checks on the listener's comprehension when addressing older partners than when addressing young partners" (32). When elderspeak was used, older participants "self-reported communication problems" that were "contrary to fact, because they actually did better as listeners and their partners had few complaints about their performance as speakers." However, Kemper indicates that "the use of elderspeak by the young partners appeared to trigger older adults' perceptions of themselves as cognitively impaired" (33). Kemper and her colleagues decided to try and "disentangle the beneficial parameters of elderspeak that enhance older listeners' comprehension from those that contribute to older adults' negative self-assessments" (33). They found (through a series of three experiments) that "it is possible to develop a form of elderspeak that benefits older adults and that does not give rise to negative self-assessments of communicative competence and is not perceived as insulting or patronizing. This form of elderspeak would provide semantic elaborations" (36). Providing semantic elaborations may give more clarity and could be a compromise for the likes of Wysocki.

Regarding under-accommodation, Kemper argues that "incomprehensible texts, such as insurance documents, health-care guidelines, and other medical and legal texts, not only fail to inform the reader but also may render the older adult vulnerable to fraud and deception if they must rely on others to inform, explain, or clarify" (38). How should these texts be fixed? Style guides such as Strunk and White's *Elements of Style*, grammar editors, and readability formulas may not improve one's chances of creating effective text. As Kemper indicates, "these prescriptions are not based on psychological models of reading nor are they validated by empirical research" (41). Citing an earlier study, Kemper argues that "older adults' reading comprehension can be enhanced by avoiding propositionally dense sentences and complex syntactic constructions" (42). The conundrum is to somehow navigate between text that might seem like an over-accommodation to the likes of Wysocki and text that would under-accommodate participants. Clearly, Kemper and Wysocki examine different kinds of designs (texts?). As the targeted audience for this text is faculty, the curriculum should address this audience as "thoughtful, patient, and intelligent," while at the same time giving straightforward information. Arriving at such a curriculum requires sophisticated rhetorical moves. We need to know more about their expectations as audience members and what works for them. Does that mean that we should create studies that reveal the efficacy of curriculum, following Kemper's strategies from cognitive psychology methodology? Perhaps. We may also observe interactions between trainers and participants or provide various manuals and explore the efficacy of certain types of textually controlled curriculum.

If we are to incorporate these design features, how will we think about an aging audience member? And what can we do to address this unified, monolithic sense of the older adult. In a culture that places value on bodies, what does it signify to take on an identity that threatens one's ability to be seen as thoughtful, patient, and intelligent enough "to make the effort"? I think research can help participants to set appropriate text level and shape the physical designs to address human factor concerns, but the challenge is to do this work while balancing cultural biases (and consequences) for admitting particular needs, because to speak about text accommodations is to raise issues familiar to disability studies.

When I first started teaching in a computer-aided classroom and using a web page for my classes, two benefits emerged. First, as an unorganized handler of paper, students suddenly saw me as much more organized, because they could access writing assignments and course information directly from the web at their convenience. Second, a shoulder injury made it extremely painful to write on chalk boards for several class periods in a row. After most days teaching, I couldn't do other work that involved arm strength, limiting my activities. With the move to a computer-aided classroom, my arm didn't bother me as much and teaching became easier. I describe this situation because teaching with computers actually made me seem more fit to do my job, both in terms of organization and basic body functioning, even though I changed neither my organization habits nor my body ability. The computer classroom was just much easier. Moving from disabilities to abilities (without significant changes in my relation to my body) was a lucky consequence.

But for others, the same classroom would feel like a move from ability to disability. Susan Wendell, in her text *The Rejected Body,* argues that "how much ability is basic, like how much ability is normal, seems to depend on how much is necessary to perform the most common tasks of daily living in a particular physical and social environment" (16) so that if we change the physical and social environment, who is able to perform and who is disadvantaged in performance may shift. Who we see as able can be redefined and then enforced both in formal and informal social cues within the organization.

Right now, in the computer classroom, I feel more powerful, more capable. If my job changes fundamentally, but the resources and social supports aren't there to help me adapt, then power dynamics shift. In our field, who is enabled or disabled by the changes in technology will affect the discipline. Susan Wendell makes an interesting connection between the pace of life and the degree to which one is seen as disabled. She argues that "when the pace of society increases, there is a tendency for more people to become disabled, not only because of physically damaging consequences of efforts to go faster, but also because fewer people can meet expectations of 'normal' performance; the physical (and mental) limitations of those who cannot meet the new pace become conspicuous and disabling" (37). Wendell argues that typically, the "public world is the world of strength, the positive (valued) body, performance and production, the non-disabled, and young adults. Weakness, illness, pain, death, and the negative (devalued) body are private, generally hidden, and often neglected" (40). We need to create research for our field that addresses human factors concerns—from textual considerations to the teaching and office conditions for faculty. MLA reports remind us that writing teachers are often without offices, without the resources. At our institution, faculty have more than most places, but we are by no means shaping ergonomically appropriate classrooms for faculty in which to learn or teach, nor are we adequately addressing the impact of the pace with which change in technology affects our perceptions of our abilities.

7

LEARNING ENVIRONMENTS

PAYING ATTENTION TO STRUCTURAL SUPPORTS

A couple of years ago, I became interested in eye tracking research, and when the opportunity to use such a machine arose, I shaped a study that would gather data on how writing faculty read web pages. It all seemed fine until I actually had to conduct the study, at which point I realized just how difficult it can be to track a person's eyes. The machinery and the set-up seem pretty easy to understand: the eye tracker follows a person's pupil, and the computer records the fixations and saccades of the reader. Although the person running the experiment monitors three or four different screens, it appears a relatively simple procedure. However, I discovered just how difficult it was when I started using the machine instead of observing a skilled graduate student conducting her studies. The challenge came in setting the eye tracking machine to individual eyes. The machine is sophisticated, but tracking a person's pupil can, at times, be impossible. For example, I couldn't figure out what to do with the person who squinted so much that her pupil was constantly obscured; another participant had impossibly tiny pupils; one person's head movements never were controlled even with a headrest; some individuals were consummate blinkers. I could go on and on with the list of challenges. Slowly learning the ins and outs, though, I started to know what to do, but by that point, my enthusiasm had waned because the lessons were learned in front of people who had agreed to participate in this study.

I should say that friends and colleagues let me practice on them before I started the study, but they couldn't possibly represent all the kinds of eyes, and I also knew, from observing others who ran studies, that they too had difficulties. They told me how they adapted to various idiosyncrasies and assured me that it merely took time to learn various tricks. Over the course of the study, I became more proficient at tracking eyes. Sometimes, it was so easy. Other times, when the pupil couldn't be tracked, I would feel myself becoming anxious and apologetic; the worry would spread perhaps because I hated not being an expert and having to figure something out while a participant waited patiently, staring at some image for too long a time. In addition to feeling like a novice, I always had the suspicion that I was a slow learner, verging on incompetent. On good days, the three or four appointments went well; as a result, I had energy to do other work. On bad days, when one or two participants' pupils required this battery of problem solving methods, I would leave the lab exhausted beyond all measure.

At the end of the study, I understood much more about how it all worked, but my fascination with eye tracking dimmed, perhaps only because my pace of mastery was much too slow, particularly given my sense of myself as a quick learner of technology. In retrospect, the experience gave me more empathy for people who struggle with technology. I've always learned programs on my own, or with minimal interaction with teachers, and although I sometimes get stuck and frustrated and have to remember to breathe and slowly figure out what I'm learning, my training is at my own pace and rarely public. When stuck, I will call and ask someone questions or attend a workshop. Usually that's all it takes. The absolute "outing" of my learning/novice status in this situation drove me batty. I blamed the technology and myself; I could not believe that I couldn't acquire the skills more quickly. Perhaps most frustrating, the only way to become more proficient always required another person to be present in order for me to pick up the skills.

Given my experience, I try to imagine what my reactions would be if suddenly my job required me to train students on how use eye trackers. Would I presume that with enough time and patience, it wouldn't be that bad? Would I start thinking about a different career? I don't know, but I return to my experience when exploring this issue of faculty development and training because it helps me to imagine what these learning situations may feel like for faculty. I like to think of myself as a smart expert, someone who has taught and read in the field long enough to be able to participate and contribute my perspectives, but the eye tracker challenged my sense of competence, making me feel like a novice.

In all honesty, the eye-tracking experience has not destabilized my world. Not much was riding on it. It was just a first—a first time of feeling less than capable with technology, feeling like I might not be able to "master" it. The ability to master it wasn't tied to my ability to make a living, wasn't necessary to keep my current position, wasn't necessary to future positions. I didn't feel like the global economy was pressing down on me, making me want to be more flexible in order to accommodate the whims of a volatile market. I just wasn't able to learn in ways that made it possible for me to maintain some sense of myself as a capable technologically astute individual.

The experience, however, reinforced my belief that we need to pay careful attention to what scholars within adult education are discovering, and we need to contribute research about faculty development for our field, particularly when technology training is connected to individuals' worries over job security. Working in a global economy, our progress takes place within a "context of wide-ranging technological, economic and political changes, linked to globalization" (Davey 96). In such a climate of "economic globalization, neoliberal economics, and market competitiveness," we may try to learn new literacies as a "means of attaining and maintaining the flexibility that is considered necessary" (Edwards and Usher 279). Flexibility is the buzz word, one that may be more difficult for people who are in the most tenuous positions, and flexibility is emphasized in such a way that it affects educational structures (Edwards, Clarke, Harrison, and Reeve 132). Edwards and Usher contend that "in a risk society, one cannot stop learning, not only in relation to work but also in relation to life more generally" and in such a situation, how we think about what we're doing can be more of a reflection of the dominant ideologies than we might realize. I'm fascinated by change, but how much of that curiosity is part of my collusion in the values that have been shaped by a trend towards globalization?

Edwards and Usher claim that the "workforce at all levels is required to think change and to have a positive attitude toward and be prepared to accept change" (278) and the pressures to adapt easily and learn new materials and take on new positions has meant that the kinds of education we desire has shifted—from "curiosity-driven" research to "learning that seeks to optimize the efficiency and effectiveness of the economic and social system" (279). I can see the tension of this kind of tradeoff in my own eye tracking situation. Initially drawn to eye tracking machines because of the ways they might inform my sense of how reading and writing happens on the web, my curiosity-driven learning shifted to one that focused on efficiency and effectiveness, because I felt the pressures of accommodating other people's time and the money available for research.

How should we shape training for faculty? Efficiency is certainly a necessity for all of us, but how much time do we allot ourselves if we place ourselves into the efficiency agenda? In my own experience, as long as no one else is involved, I can play in the curiosity novice position for as long as necessary, but as soon as a deadline looms (e.g., Learn Flash for a conference presentation), curiosity vanishes. I'm left with my self-imposed measures of efficiency. However, if play and curiosity remain in the mix, I learn despite my anxiety over the deadline. For individuals who cannot keep play in, or who cannot meet the deadlines, one of the possibilities is to just opt out. For some this can be a significant opting out—retirement. Particularly in the academy, we need to address both the desires for retirement and the challenges inherent in the life cycle. At different points in our lives we are more available for training and development. Personal lives shape the ability to be present, and we need to be cognizant of the multiple pressures writing faculty face. In our department, with a predominantly female population over forty, we have to be aware of family obligations and the squeeze many of our faculty feel. If we are to be humane in the midst of the pressure-filled environment, we need to figure ways of attaining goals that fit with both the individual's and the department's needs, recognizing that at times, those goals may be disparate.

In the midst of a life cycle that is increasingly "distributing learning, work, and leisure" more evenly "over the entire course of one's life time" (Kressley and Huebschmann 839), but which affects many in this sense of an increasingly blurred boundary between "personal time and space of the home" and work (Howell, Carter and Schied 121), we may want to work carefully to determine faculty curriculum. Rossiter suggests that thinking of life courses in terms of the narrative we want to create can help to acknowledge "the interconnectedness of individual and cultural narratives" because, as Rossiter argues, "individual life narratives are situated within a myriad of overlapping familial, religious, socioeconomic and cultural contexts" (65). We may be able to shape our narratives to create possible life trajectories, fitting within the cultures' expectations, which, as Rossiter argues, "has a pool of acceptable narratives, a set of stories and story forms, through which human action and intent are interpreted, explained, and understood" (66).

We know many stories for the population of instructors, adjuncts, teaching assistants, and faculty who teach first-year writing; many participate in a larger culture that expects different roles for men and women, and women often feel as if they have two full-time jobs, the work in both the public and the private sphere (Stalker 289). As Settersten and Lovegreen remind us, "women still shoulder the major responsibility for the caring and raising of children, and these responsibilities strongly condition women's educational attainment and enrollment and their attachment to the labor market" (509). In addition, "the position of women in the labor market is still one of marked disadvantage relative to men, even *net* of all qualifications, skills, family roles and responsibilities" (509). These expectations fit with life course and work course narratives. As Settersten and Lovegreen suggest, the ways of seeing these differences in male and female life courses may be to mark the flexibility in women's spheres and the very rigid boxes of male work (507). Although Settersten and Lovegreen admit that "surely many men must desire more flexibility in their work patterns," the reality remains that "pension policies often work against, and even penalize those who take flexible pathways" (512). In the midst of the gendered tensions, Rossiter's calls for narrative reorientation need to be addressed. In this literacy work, there needs to be room for exploring the narrative options and finding humane ways of navigating always shifting work and family pressures.

Two main tensions seem at stake in training and faculty development, when drawing from adult education scholarship. First, individuals perform within economic frameworks, ones that shape the choices regarding life course trajectories. As a result, faculty may feel the pressure to be efficient and effective in learning new material and may wish for more of an emphasis on curiosity-driven research, though this emphasis may not touch all faculty. One of my friends, for example, was struggling to learn how to conduct research on-line. She was not very trusting of on-line sources. After she had convinced herself that she wouldn't be able to master a search engine such as google, she became curious about what had happened to the people with whom she attended high school, and in a matter of days, her abilities to perform on-line searches were dramatically improved. Although the efficiency/effective pressure might move other faculty members, it was curiosity that shaped my friend's learning. With secure job status, her motivations are different than those who need to be most "flexible" in this economy. Second, training within a framework that draws on the expertise of faculty makes more sense than separating technology training from their knowledge of writing instruction. When technology training is separated, then faculty may be more likely to be treated (and think of themselves) as novices.

Barbara Daley studied expert and novice nurses and found that novices learn by studying a concept, but are affected by fear, their mistakes, and their need for validation, which leads to contingent learning (139). Experts, in contrast, ground their learning in clients' needs and practice settings, which leads to active integration of concepts through assimilation with experience, through differentiation of experience, and through dialog and sharing of experience, which lead to constructivist learning processes (141). In Daley's description, the experts process information through conversation with other experts, testing new information against old knowledge. When training for faculty happens in a centralized location, for the whole campus, faculty may be split off from their expertise status. Even when the training is discipline specific, if the technology overwhelms, faculty may retreat to a novice position. In addition, the novice position has different impact on faculty, based on their status, and may be more complicated for older, more established faculty to navigate. How do we mitigate the fears associated with technology that place a person in the position of thinking they can break the machine, or make a too public a gaffe, and somehow bring in the possibility of combining expertise with novice situations?

What we may want to explore also is how to bring older participants into faculty curriculum design with more of an awareness of some of the issues that may be creating gaps between those who do technologically rich literacies and those who don't. In Yeatts, Folts and Knapp's article on work adaptation, they indicate that there are better and worse strategies for encouraging work adaptation, defining it as "the continuous and dynamic process by which an individual seeks to establish a complementary, reciprocal relationship, or fit with his or her job" (567). Although they are generally describing corporate work environments in which employees are trained and work differently, their insights may be of use to us. They remind us that "recently redesigned jobs often are more demanding than the more traditional jobs they replace" (569) and suggest that workers may be worried that they "will be unable to learn the new methods, procedures, or techniques required" (570). Workers, according to Yeatts et al., often opt to retire when they perceive "a redesigned work environment . . . as increasing stress, repetitiveness or physical requirements" (571). Changes in jobs objectives can affect the sense of value—in terms of seniority counting or "privileges based solely on tenure" (571). These changes can also affect a person's sense of her influence. "Long-termed employees may believe that they have earned the right to have more influence over workplace decisions" and "shorter-tenured employees" who may be seen by management as more knowledgeable may face resistance from long-termed employees (578). Changes in structure and emphasis can lead some long-term employees to see the shifts as a demotion of their value (576).

Although this research may not be exactly in line with academic experiences and the particular population demographics of writing instructors, there are echoes in comments people make about shifting values/attentions in the field. Who can shape the directions for first-year writing program outcomes may fit into these kinds of voiced concerns. How does a community adapt to provost, president, or chancellor level directives to offer courses that integrate technologically rich literacies? Should longer-term employees shape expectations and outcomes? If the new outcomes require faculty to adapt to new technological demands, how will individuals perceive those expectations? If I have always taught writing in a traditional classroom, if I have difficulty seeing computer screens in the computer classrooms, if I fear that I will make errors in front of my students, I may see these shifts in expectations as threatening my ability to do my job, increasing my levels of stress.

Yeatts et al. suggest some possible strategies to shift the negative responses. They argue that any redesign needs to have a "detailed and carefully presented account of just what changes will be made and their anticipated effects on the individual employees and the organization as a whole" (573). Any training should follow "available research," which "suggests that older workers learn best when they can learn at their own pace, when they are allowed to learn with their age peers, and when the anxieties associated with learning something new are addressed" (575). If the training is provided "far in advance of when new skills are needed," if "additional learning opportunities for those who desire them" are provided, and if administrations/managers are "sympathetic and make explicit efforts to help workers during a job transition," and "publicize achievements and contributions of older workers," changes can be more successful (575-76). In addition, "coworker support can mitigate the effects of job stress and anxiety" (576).

Their recommendations seem like common sense, yet I don't often encounter training and development workshops shaped in these ways. Often, we fail to know what changes are to be made and what effects there will be on the individual employees. We don't figure out what new skills we need and set up an adequate time line for ourselves. Nor do we set up learning groups that are made up of age peers. And rarely do we establish a conversation about or attempt to address "the anxieties associated with learning something new." Part of research can include better practices that address and give time to participants who come to training and development. In academe, one walks the tension between encouraging the perk of job autonomy that draws many of us to the profession and the necessity of teaching to shared objectives. But we may need to find out the best practices for establishing goals that are collective and goals that are individual, and to collectively and individually set out a time line that fits with the individual's sense of what can be accomplished. That time line might be five years or five months, but we don't do this kind of individualized work currently at my institution. Not only do we not take into account a feasible strategy for setting goals, we don't navigate the issues at stake for participants who feel threatened or uninterested or bored by the new literacies.

We would benefit from a humane approach to shifting objectives, and we're likely to progress much more quickly if we adopt certain methods for learning over others. In adult education discussions, one of the obvious possibilities for learning is to play off of existing communities of learners and networks that already function for the people involved. "Networks are considered a knowledge resource" and they interact with "identity resources—cognitive and affective attributes; self-confidence," and so forth (Balatti and Falk 285). A network, for Balatti and Falk, can be "as small as two" (285). The idea of existing communities and networks seems an obvious resource for us. One doesn't have to look far to see the roles networks play in writing teachers' lives. We see the gravitations of people towards each other—towards like-minded colleagues who share teaching issues/concerns. These networks could, perhaps be tapped; however, the research strategies for such tapping are complicated by several issues, not the least of which is an inability to navigate these warm concepts of community or network critically. Communities are challenging to research because the term of "community" or "network" "lacks rigor and is too inclusive to be analytically useful" (St. Clair 6). Not only are they hard to define, the politics of communities and networks are not without their troubling sides. People are included and excluded based on a group's sense of social hierarchy. As Billett argues, "workplace cliques and affiliations serve to distribute opportunities to participate and learn by affecting access to guidance and prized activities" (20), so that networks wind up "protecting and promoting the particular interests and affiliations of groups or individuals within the workplace" (20). This means that research that attempts to integrate networks needs to be thoughtful about the multiple competing interests at stake in training and development. A focus on relation matters, as we may be able to figure out what kind of "relationship we want to develop" and how we shape these relations (St. Clair 13).

The existing networks and hierarchies often will shape the kinds of learning groups that are formed, and strategic design of a learning group takes into account existing traditions and the existing pool of acceptable narratives. Poell, VanDerKrogt and Warmerdam overview types of learning groups and the values/ideologies they reflect. They start by defining a "learning project" as comprised of three issues: "(a) learning group which involves a number of employees who are prepared to conduct a range of learning activities together; (b) a learning theme representing an issue relevant to the daily work of the participants about which they want to learn;

and (c) a set of learning activities, taking place both in formal and informal settings" (29). Learning groups "combine individual and collective learning activities" (30). After setting up the terms, they move to the types of learning networks: liberal, vertical, horizontal, and external learning networks. In liberal networks

> individual learners organize their own learning process and create their own learning programs. They decide what they want to learn and organize a loosely coupled network of people to help them achieve it. The learners manage the coordination and control of learning. The learning program consists of individual activities and is relatively unstructured. (33)

To contrast,

> in the vertical learning network, centralized and hierarchy play an important role in the coordination and control of learning. The management and educators of the organization draw up policy plans, design learning programs and supervise the learners. The learning program is linearly planned and function-oriented.

In thinking about how we typically learn our technology at my local institution, it is often more like vertical learning than the liberal network. Different from these two types of learning groups is "the horizontal network" in which learning groups

> develop learning programs together incrementally. In these cooperative activities, a lot of attention is given to the development of shared norms and views on learning. The learning program is problem-oriented and integrated with daily work.

This type of group seems to combine the best of the liberal model with more meta discourse that may be beneficial to writing faculty. Finally, they point to the last kind of learning network, an external one: in this paradigm

> actors outside the organization are crucial. External inspiration (e.g., from the scientific community or a professional association) has a great impact on this learning network. (33)

These four types of learning networks help us to see some possible alternatives, and they also suggest the kinds of ideologies that we might find in various kinds of writing instruction programs.

In my community college job as an adjunct writing teacher, travel funds requests were granted only after extensive individual faculty development forms were completed, which repeatedly asked for some sense of an integration of goals that would benefit students. Only when I had a development plan could the request be granted, because only then could they see how spending money for this particular conference would contribute to the development that would be of direct benefit to the students/college. In the training that I attended while a part of that institution, I often had this sense of a vertical learning network that felt similar to this travel worksheet requirement; I was trained in what they decided I needed to know only if they could see a direct link to students—as if one wouldn't discover many implications for teaching after the fact. As a teaching assistant, I was also similarly trained in these ways (and trained others). With a large gaggle of novice teaching assistants, necessity sometimes meant having to say "follow these guidelines." In my current position, with almost exclusively full-time writing faculty, we are a community that decides which values to share. This is not easy work, but I think our situation affords opportunities to explore learning communities and networks that might function more like a liberal learning network.

Not only do we need to think about how to shape the learning networks, but we also need to consider space and time and establish situations that are more conducive to people learning from one another. Lohman, studying teachers and their opportunities for learning, claims that "organizational environments influence the desire or ability of individuals to engage in informal learning" (84). She maintains that space and time play a role in how well we can "foster informal learning" (85). Keeping with this sense of community and collaboration, she points to scheduling issues that limit opportunities for teachers of the same subject to interact with one another in informal settings (88), including "environmental inhibitors to informal learning" which include learning methods, environmental influences, teaching responsibilities, learning sources, personal influences and personal potency.[1] Her lists may overwhelm, but are necessary to research that helps us determine what might aid in faculty development and training.

---

[1] Potential "environmental inhibitors to informal learning" include **learning methods**: "collaboration, formal training, independent research, individual experimentation, mentoring, observing, reflecting on past experiences, role playing, sharing resources, and talking." She marks **environmental influences**: "administrator's behaviors, availability of time, community perception of teachers, competing goals, cultural norms, departmental offices, financial resources, impact of technology,

In Lohman's analysis, taking into consideration all of these factors, one can see that some of the barriers may be more easily eradicated. For example, if a network of faculty decide to learn together, or if a department wants to facilitate informal learning, they might take a look at the schedules of faculty, at the placement of offices, at the accessibility to resources, and then start to reorganize schedules, offices, and resources so that faculty are more inclined to consult one another and to take up new learning. A network of faculty who want to learn together might be able to request similar teaching schedules so that the training and development schedule wouldn't preclude individuals' abilities to participate.

One must not only pay attention to the timing and location of individuals in the work space but also to the ergonomics of the environment. After I started reading in human factors research, I started watching my colleagues' bodies as they navigated computers. Although only a couple of the people I know will complain about the computer classrooms and the challenges they have accommodating the hardware, just watching bodies and the contortions people go through can tell us a lot about how comfortable our work environments are. Many of my friends with bifocals sit at the computer in positions that I find uncomfortable to look at, but they wouldn't complain. Neither would I. I suppose we could argue that we don't complain because of the discriminatory practices regarding disabilities, or our own internalization of those phobias; we are worried that we are aging,

---

incentives and rewards, instructional assignments, meetings, physical aspects of building, policies and procedures, school schedule, size of student enrollment, student attributes, teacher participation in decision making (high and low), teacher evaluation, the changing world, grade level" (88). From environmental influences, she moves to **teaching responsibilities**: "instructional content; instructional materials and resources, instructional strategies; extra- and cocurricular activities; school duties; school/district management; parent involvement; delivering lessons; evaluating learning; managing classroom; mentoring and developing teachers; motivating students" (88). **Learning sources** include administrators; existing information sources, other staff, people outside school, professional development activities outside school in and out of the school district, students, teachers work group membership. She turns then to **personal influences** that shape learning: age, applied focus; autonomy, commitment, educational background, educational philosophy, expertise, flexibility, gender, initiative, interpersonal skills, love of reading, openness to change, organizational skills, patience, procrastination, readiness to learn, self-concept, supervisory skills, teaching experience. She has a last category—**learning potency,** and describes three types of people: enhancers, inhibitors, and catalysts of learning (88).

that these ailments might one day lead to more disabilities. I find it interesting that we don't facilitate the navigation of body needs, making the shifts in our bodies' abilities signify more than they should.

If we're setting up environments that are smart for learning, we shouldn't place people in the position of having to request special materials; we should ask them to select from options, resources that will facilitate their experiences without making these into abilities or disabilities. We should watch faculty and students in computer classrooms, articulate the problems of design, and change the rooms to better meet faculty and student needs, so that faculty don't even need to realize that they have particular needs that come because of eyes that can not easily see screens, or hands that cannot easily adjust to ergonomically challenged keyboards, or timing that doesn't fit with the mouse speeds set by young engineers and computer lab technicians.

This chapter suggests some of the issues that might be at stake in current training dynamics—from expert/novice experiences to the type of learning networks—and how we might develop better learning networks based on informal relationships. Multiple concerns play a role in people's abilities to accumulate new literacies, from the kinds of texts we create (and their readability to those involved) to body movement requirements. We would do well to study each of these as part of a whole. How we decide to conduct research will be shaped by our own enculturations into research design and also by our local situation.

8

CONCLUSIONS

RESEARCH AS PEDAGOGY

Scholars are postulating something much more substantive about narrative: namely, that social life is itself storied and that narrative is an ontological condition of social life. Their research is showing that stories guide action; that people make sense of what has happened and is happening to them by attempting to assemble or in some way to integrate these happenings within one or more narratives; and that people are guided to act in certain ways, and not others, on the basis of the projections, expectations, and memories derived from a multiple but ultimately limited repertoire of available social, public, and cultural narratives. (Somers qtd in Thomas 613-614)

In Barbara Kingsolver's novel, *The Poisonwood Bible*, a fool of a preacher man drags his family into an African world they could never survive were it not for the kindness of the existing community, though the father remains blissfully unaware of their generosity. This ignorant man is the initial focus for the story, and readers, together with his family and the village inhabitants, must endure his Sunday sermons. On these occasions, Kingsolver's narrator emphasizes the gap between what the preacher thinks he says and the translation. When the father speaks for himself, he often mispronounces words, radically altering the meaning. He says "Jesus;" they hear "poisonwood," a dangerous plant that causes skin irritation. In addition to his ignorance of language, he also fails to imagine those to whom he speaks as anything other than evil sinners, ripe for conversion. The text lacks subtlety. This unfortunate person reminds us of the horrors of colonization: his is a story of religious imposition, of reinscribing raced and gendered injustices.

Readers may easily despise and dismiss Kingsolver's character, but for me his image contrasts with more complicated preachers in my missionary childhood, men who were more loveable and harder to untangle than this ignorant preacher man. Though I am uneasy with missionary work, I find Kingsolver's text unsatisfying. Instead of either of these types, I want a preacher and translator who understand that preaching through translation means creating cadences that persuade people to change perspectives despite the fragmentary gaps of in-between time, pausing, waiting for the translation. I want to know that they are aware of the sophisticated rhetorical challenge of this type of collaboration. However, in Kingsolver's text, the most complicated task of preaching via translation is left to the most simplistic of men; our allegiance rests with the man who must willingly mistranslate so as to keep the missionary safe from the ire of the community, the person who knows enough of two cultures to understand what the preacher might say, were he more sophisticated.

I suppose one could argue that we're all involved in translation, in missed translations. We try to convey ideas that aren't quite fully formed in language, searching for words, images, space that will convey emotions, perspectives, challenges. The gaps, the mistranslations, the disrupted cadences, the words held under erasure already have a rich tradition in critical theory (see Graham for a starting point). Nothing new here. Translation involved in conversions may be a little less routine, though it is hard in postmodern times to chase translations that aren't about conversions/confessions. I often make this claim: that much of teaching slides around this issue of conversion in part because of traditions around confessions (Foucault 59-67), in part because of the definitions of epiphany. Those "aha" moments, those interpellation moments (Althusser), are the fodder of conversion. Or perhaps they are the fodder for the likes of me, inundated with the evangelical traditions of a United States family abroad such that I cannot see my work without always filtering through these larger motifs of judeo-christian rituals (see Haraway too, 51, 61).

I worry that the position of the all knowing computers and writing person may parallel these images of preacher men. In conversations about what literacies will matter in our field, I want to suggest (and explore in research) the idea that people with less investment in changing literacies really can't imagine why these shifts matter—can't see a "there" there, can't see shifts there. When one group says "Jesus," the other group hears "poisonwood." Or when one group says on-line multimedia "essays," the other group hears "abandoning the craft of writing." These kinds of misses are rich in the histories of conversion that always make me uneasy. One group, the ones who might be seen as basic writers, are placed in the position of not having the right wisdom. Someone from outside, from the land of knowledge, addresses these ignorant sinners. Depending on the degree of enlightenment, the ones presumed to know may or may not be able to form translations within the values of the group. When curriculum is shaped within this frame, the potential for colonization increases; the situation requires a powerful and a powerless group, requires the imposition of values. This paradigm may also include the tired frustration of people who are placed in the role of translators, whether they want it or not, though this is a read from one perspective, one sympathetic to those who feel imposed upon (on either side of this imagined transaction of knowledge, of power). To return to the quotation cited earlier from Eve Sedgwick:

> knowledge is not itself power although it's a magnetic field of power, ignorance and opacity collude or compete with knowledge in mobilising the flows of energy, desire, goods, meanings, persons. If Monsieur Mitterrand knows English but Mr Reagan lacks, as he did lack French, it is the urbane Monsieur Mitterrand who must negotiate in an acquired tongue, the ignorant Mr Reagan who may dilate in his native one. (23)

For many in the position of translating/preaching, perhaps the barrier is raised because they would prefer not to be placed in a complicated negotiation about changing literacies, or perhaps this is only my response. Nonetheless, the challenge comes in taking the basic writer on one side and the translator on the other and working around to a more collaborative image that we can hold, one that situates neither party in troubling locations. I want to suggest that participants could come to some theory about how power functions in the local situation and shape responses/actions that move the power around in ways conducive to group identity, to create through cultural disruptions a migration away from existing strategies for knowledge acquisition that occur within troubling hierarchies.

FINDING METAPHORS FOR PEDAGOGY:
A RICKETY BRIDGE

All too often those who can teach or lead with authority are armored against new learning, while those who are open to new learning are made diffident about expressing what they do know by the very fact that they deem it tentative. (Bateson 73)

How can one create a performative pedagogy in the West which refuses the acquisitive model of power-knowledge operative everywhere in institutions of "higher learning"? How can one invent a pedagogy for disappearance and loss and not for acquisition and control? How can one teach the generative power of misunderstanding in a way they will (almost) understand? And who are "they" anyway?" (Phelan 173)

Misunderstanding as a political and pedagogical telos can be a dangerous proposition, or it invites the belligerent refusal to learn or love at all. This is not what I am arguing for. *It is an attempt to walk (and live) on the rackety bridge between self and other—and not the attempt to arrive at one side or the other—that we discover real hope."* (Phelan 174)

Transference on "the subject presumed to know"—the analyst or the teacher—may provide a countertransference on the latter's part. The analytic or pedagogical situation may thus degenerate into an imaginary mirror game of love and hate, where each of the participants would unconsciously enact past conflicts and emotions, unwarranted by the current situation and disruptive with respect to the real issues, unsettling the topic stakes of analysis or education. (Felman 86)

Accumulating literacies is always a dialogic act, and according to Shoshana Felman, our desire for dialogue is our hope of discovering the Other, the "subject presumed to know" (84). Felman speaks to the complications of learning relationships. What I want to suggest in designing research is that when we categorize participants as ignorant or when we categorize teachers as those presumed to know, we cannot shape a pedagogy that addresses our needs as adult learners. People have multiple responses to being placed in the position of someone presumed to know, from enjoying that sense of omnipotence or competence to the diffidence that Mary Catherine Bateson describes. The position of the one presumed to know has to be abandoned if we are to "invent a pedagogy for disappearance and loss and not for acquisition and control" (Phelan above). Such teaching is not easily accomplished, but I do think that we can still create disruptions locally, disruptions that negate proclivities towards acquisition and control. If the stories we tell shape the "repertoire of available social, public, and cultural narratives" (Somers), the imaginary domains we inhabit, then a rackety bridge may serve as an image for the rhetorical situation that I'm proposing. Blurring the "sides" of rhetor and audience may allow for expertise to exist next to new learning.

However, four issues may cause difficulties: first, existing power structures may resist this image; second, our own relations to/histories with education may disrupt learning; third, theories of literacy as they apply to "adult learners" may compete with what I'm trying to imagine; and finally, our attitudes towards aging (and our other accompanying identity categories) may shape assumptions.

First, several issues shape the ability to reimagine curriculum design. Perhaps most difficult is the institutional and departmental climate. In my dissertation, I wrote about the challenges English departments faced in the 1980s and 1990s and how difficult it is for some institutions to shift values, to create a different definition of an English department. Battles are waged in such situations over the locus of power and shifting access to resources. When funding is given for technology, we still need to understand/assess how resources are distributed and how decisions are made. Agreeing on change requires attentiveness to existing structures for all parties. If technology-based literacies have been marginalized, fed through one or two people, the department needs to evaluate the current structure and decide how it wants to shape the lines of power. Should the locus of power rest with one or two people or with other paradigms? Which structures are most likely to lead to the most thoughtful adoption of technology (and more collaborative learning)? What structures preclude a rackety bridge? What structures can negate the inclinations towards an "acquisitive model of power-knowledge?" (Phelan, above).

In addition to institutional and departmental climates, individuals' reactions to challenges are disparate. Throughout life courses, individuals may seek out job situations that play to strengths but that don't necessarily allow them to experience learning differently or to desire learning. Mary Catherine Bateson tells the story of Einstein and Eisenhower encountering an exhibit on optical illusions, one in which, "the visitor was invited to touch various points with a stick, but because of deliberately distorted clues of perspective the stick kept missing." The two men's reactions, according to the story, are described as follows: Eisenhower "lost his temper when he visited, threw down the stick, and refused to continue." In contrast, Einstein "was fascinated when he encountered the same errors, using them to explore further" (73). Bateson makes sense of these two reactions by pointing out that "the two men had clearly found their ways to greatness in the niches that fit their temperaments, but they were also shaped by the conventions of the world in which they worked" (74). These anecdotes echo Dweck's research on motivation described in Chapter Four.

One's relationship to education plays a role. We each enter with our identities in tow, with all the baggage of educational experiences, with all our strategies for making sense of new situations and our awareness of our identities as performers. Some of us may be delighted with the rhetorical situation in which we are learners, and those presumed to know give us much that we soak up, but that's not the case for others. These ways of being are then complicated by our individual living. Faculty development and training happens in the middle of people's busy lives. Already stretched thin, often feeling overworked, people hear that technologically rich literacies are desired by some in the discipline, but also deans and provosts and may or may not imagine a way to heed the call, the interpellation. They also may not approve of the changes. The rickety bridge metaphor may be resisted by multiple participants but for disparate educational/historical reasons.

Third, what it means to perform literate acts shifts with time and changes in technology. To see one's literacies age and to address one's ability to acquire new literacies within the framework of aging may be overwhelming. We have, for many years, understood that there are multiple literacies (Cope and Kalantzis, Cushman, Kress, Luke, Wysocki, etc.), that the literacies advocated within the academy or within Western culture are not easily morphed onto other cultures, that colonization occurs with literacy instruction (Freire; Fox; Street; Stuckey; Taylor). In a very short time, technological change will shift (or already has shifted) the definitions of literacy for the mainstream composition faculty at many institutions, and when faculty must acquire these changing literacies, when we start to expect that a writing class will automatically include technological components such as a listserv or a courseware component, when we see writing classrooms move from including web page instruction to quick time movies or flash, then it becomes a complicated situation because some people who feel very comfortable and confident teaching writing suddenly consider themselves less than comfortable and competent, and may experience the required literacies as a sort of colonization on their bodies.

In this description, for those whose literacies are aging and those whose literacy accumulations place them among the ones presumed to know, the possibilities for trouble are clear. In the situation of the ones presumed to know, the temptation may be to draw unnecessary conclusions about others' resistance to change. What those presumed to know might do, in situations where faculty must accumulate new literacies, with rarely the time allotted to enable literacy acquisition, is to blame the people who cannot quickly (or slowly) learn the technology-based literacies, instead of looking towards the system and the problems that make it difficult for individuals to understand why they would benefit from different literacies and impede their ability to acquire the needed information (see Brodkey). This tendency would also parallel work in literacy studies that seeks to understand why the frames of literacy have been shaped as they have by the popular press. In such stories, "issues of poverty and unemployment can be turned into questions about why individuals failed to learn literacy at school, or continue to refuse remedial attention as adults, thus diverting blame from institutions to individuals, from power structures to personal morality" (Street 125).

When we shape our research, we must be careful not to repeat the literacy gaffes that reflect larger cultural attitudes towards literacy. Examining literacy from the perspective of technological changes and challenges and the complications associated with aging, the conversations address a surprising population in the academy—one that has traditionally been associated with power. A full professor surely doesn't have to bother with literacy training, but individuals are encountering changing expectations. How will they make sense of that pressure to accumulate? What have we learned about adult literacy programs that could be useful here?

We also may find that faculty involved in literacy accumulation have one set of standards for their students and another one for themselves. For example, my writing classroom is shaped by assumptions/beliefs about how we acquire literacies. However, the teaching principles I hold for others are not necessarily the ones I subscribe to for myself when I am in the position of learner. I'm none too patient when my pace of learning is slow. If immediate results are poor, I have had to learn how relax about the speed at which I figure out new knowledge. When researching others' experiences, I listen to hear if alphabet literacy is highest in the hierarchy; I ask questions about educational experiences with language learning and other literacies acquired in youth and in adult living. If a person holds one set of literacy theories for students, and another set for him or herself, those attitudes/expectations need to be explored and addressed.

Larger writing program questions also exist: How do we give first-year composition teachers autonomy in classrooms, yet encourage the teaching of shifting literacies? How do we avoid involving ourselves in actions that might seem colonizing to those who cannot imagine that these shifting literacies matter. Not all of us will agree on what kinds of literacies should count, and many exhortations already exist that suggest the need to be cautious in embracing new technologies (Barton, Charney, Dobrin, Faigley, Haas and Neuwirth, to name only a few).

In this text, I've tried to put forth some pretty standard beliefs about literacy that we as a community might find familiar: that literate beliefs shape our actual pedagogical strategies, that they determine how members are included or excluded, that we may or may not allow room for a wide range of definitions for what counts as literacy. Our literacy training often explores the pedagogical frameworks and tries to move outside the paradigm of an all-knowing teacher who distributes knowledge to students. I've pointed to issues that prohibit movement—the Basic Writer image, for example. I've suggested the power dynamics at play in a paradigm that includes a rhetor who presumes to know and basic writers who are marginalized participants within the university structure.

In thinking about ways to gather data that might give us clues about literacy beliefs, I think the best method from my experiences is to allow individuals many different opportunities to answer questions that ask them to address literate practices. In the research Duffey and I conducted on aging and training, participants were asked in writing, in focus groups, in interviews and follow-up interviews for positions on literacy. We would ask questions about experience in these different venues, and the combined answers, taking into account contextual influences, shaped what we understood about each individual. From these various venues, then, we could gather a sense of a person's life history and experiences from oral interviews, their sense of learning practices in collaboration with their peers, and their assessments in writing, which offered possibilities for more reflective thinking. Because we had the luxury of these different qualitative methods, we were able to ask an extensive range of questions and were able to gather a better sense of what might be motivating individuals to hold the attitudes they presented.

One of my biggest points of curiosity is the imaginary individuals evoke. What we found interesting in this group is that all of the participants had negative experiences with training and development, and when we asked them to tell us about images they have of themselves in these situations, they confirmed the impulse to feel like basic writers. Although they didn't use those exact terms, they emphasized the feeling of marginalization and infantilization. The repetitions of negative experiences were daunting to consider. As I make sense of the basic writer image, as I review the stories these people told of their experiences with computers and writing, I wonder about future research. Could we collectively come up with images that would be more useful for participants to hold as they navigate the learning situations?

Given the complications of faculty development and training, the multiple positions we occupy, the strategies we have for negotiating our labor requirements, we need to craft (and draw on existing) models that allow for people to have more of a voice in what they learn and in how they learn it. This is not a new idea—for many years our field has explored different pedagogical approaches, and has tried to shift the rhetorical situation of the classroom away from the authoritarian teacher model (Bartholomae; Bruffee; Freire; Lindemann; Lunsford and Ede; Shor; etc.). This idea is certainly evoked in adult learning materials and in discussions of computers and writing (see early on, Barker and Kemp, Handa, Kaplan). So long as institutions continue to approach faculty training and development and the accumulation of new literacies with familiar—but not necessarily useful—skill and drill models, interventions are needed.

The lack of adequate faculty curriculum design should not be the most dominant factor in the writing program objectives that we adopt; instead, we should do our research so that we can create curriculum for writing faculty that allows for the feasibility of literacy shifts in program development. If we set up the paradigm to be colonized/colonizer or presumed to know/ignorant, we cannot arrive at the kinds of collaborations I envision, nor, I would argue, at the literacies we envision teaching. Research on faculty training should draw on our best practices, and we have many valid research traditions. However, our research also needs to address aging.

The information gathered in this text suggests the extensive range of existing research on aging available in other fields. It may help to summarize the material reviewed in this text in order to understand the full range of choices available to a researcher when thinking about how to design research about aging.

From Chapter Two: Defining Age

Life Course Questions:

- What presumptions about life-course decisions do participants hold?

- What roles have subjects adopted over the course of their lives and how have those roles shaped their relation to work?
- What life course expectations/patterns/interpretations do individuals hold?
- What attitudes do they hold about learning new literacies? Are those correlated to their sense of life-course expectations?

Chronological Ages/Life-Course Questions:

- Do they evaluate themselves based on accomplishments met by certain ages?
- Do participants have a sense of expectations for particular chronological ages?
- Do their bosses or students or colleagues have expectations based on chronological age?

Individual Interpretation of Age Identity

- How old does an individual think she is? How old do others think she is?
- Are individuals aware of the trends and patterns that they fit into because they were born into particular historical contexts?
- What kinds of conceptions of time are important to participants?

From Chapter Three: Stereotyping and Aging

Tapping Identity Constructions and Stereotyping

- What metaphors are evoked by participants regarding literacy accumulation, and how are we to interpret those metaphors in terms of stereotyping and aging?
- What bodily changes do we employ to disguise aging?
- How do people make sense of this category once they're in it, or when they're not yet in it?

Investigating Our Stereotypes

- What implicit and explicit stereotypes about aging do we (and others who read us) hold?

- Do students read us as old? Do they categorize us in ways similar to Hummert's research?

Manipulating Stereotypes

- Can we evoke stereotypes, and if so, will we learn more about the degree to which infantilization occurs?
- What role might positive and negative priming play in our research?
- Are colleagues treated differently based on unexamined assumptions?
- Are social clocks contributing to workplace performance evaluations?

Mortality

- What role does mortality play in our reactions/responses? Do we adopt positions more in keeping with our worldview when reminded of our mortality?
- Do we engage in distancing behavior, separating ourselves from aging Others?

From Chapter Five: Women and Aging (or Intertwining Aging Categories)

The Personal and the Professional Choices:

- What are the career trajectories for women? (gather caregiving histories, including elder and grandchild care.)
- What background finances do we want to consider: income, family income, obligations, financial planning, inheritance, debt, savings, etc.
- How much family history is desired: Divorce, deaths, child birth complications, migrations, disabilities, and so forth.
- What kind of partner choices—and division of labor at home—exist?
- Will we check for cumulative (dis)advantages?
- Is there work loss due to illness, health care costs, medication expenses?

*What Impact Do These Personal/Professional Choices Have
on Interpretations of Women or Their Interpretations of Themselves?*

- Assumptions regarding caregiving—who should provide it?
- Does position/title matter in terms of correlations to learning curve?
- What role does a teaching career play in identity construction (i.e., crucial, a side job with family career first, etc.)?
- What are individuals' self-evaluations regarding life-course progress?
- How do participants' perceptions of one another's caregiving decisions shape responses to one another?
- What are the perceptions of students, colleagues, and administrators regarding competence of male versus female employees, of old versus young, and so forth?

From Chapter Six: Aging Bodies

Overall Concerns

- To what degree does a reluctance to discuss aging shape research design?
- What kinds of curriculum decisions will we make based on aging information—what kinds of texts will we create?
- Can we create on-line documents that use data to assess (based on input) the skill level and retrieve appropriate text?
- How will we assess the ergonomic challenges of learning/teaching spaces?

Decisions About Testing Body Abilities

- How much information do we gather regarding vision—acuity, contrast, visual field, eye movements?
- What kinds of motor coordination tests would we like to include?
- How many cognitive tests: assessing text comprehension, measuring distraction, expertise, structure, inference load?
- How much health history and medication information do we need?

- What physical challenges are participants facing?

From Chapter Seven: Adult Education Research

How Does New Learning Contribute to Identity Stability

- What role does expertise play in our current learning situations and are we creating situations in which participants are stripped of their expertise?
- What are individuals' perspectives on the degree to which new literacies contribute to or take away from their ability to "fit" within the department?
- Do new literacies alter the sense of a person's value, his or her seniority?
- Do people feel like they're losing their influence/value?

Financial Pressures

- How will we assess each participant's sense of risk and participation in economic structures?
- To what degree can we assess the pressure people feel to be efficient and curious in their learning?
- How are the changing working conditions (blurring of life course trajectories, blurring of work/home spaces) shaping learning?
- Do new literacies make the workplace situation more demanding?

What Kinds Of Learning Paradigms Should We Create?

- Do teachers see the anticipated effects of these changes?
- Are teachers allowed to learn at their own pace, with age peers and with opportunities to address "anxieties associated with learning something new" (Yeatts et al. 575)
- What kinds of networks exist and can they be tapped?
- What kind of learning paradigms exist?
- How will we assess Lohman's five categories: environmental influences; teaching responsibilities; learning sources; personal influences; and learning potency?

Age plays into the individual's assessment of his or her position in the existing power structure, his or her need to learn, and the literacy traditions evoked as (she) encounters new material. A researcher must decide, given the population, how he or she will try to assess older participants. For example, should the researcher try to understand how individuals make sense of their own age. Do they have certain expectations for particular ages in terms of influence (seniority, for example); would they prefer to spend their time elsewhere? Some people have a sense that their time is limited even early in their lives; others start to conserve energy as they age, realizing that priorities determine what they will learn. Research should decide whether and how to tap into the individual's sense of the relation between age and the energy available for new learning, because that individual's assessment may shape action.

In addition, aging research in our field should attempt to understand how life-course trajectories are intertwined with chronological age expectations and cohort traditions, because these issues influence individuals' responses to changing literacy requirements. Mentoring texts for new faculty often describe situations in which junior and senior colleagues find themselves in conflict. Disparate cohort enculturations within a field mark changes in values and paradigms. Those in the field may have significant differences in their responses to these shifts, creating complicated navigations for both younger and older faculty (and/or for faculty who share cohort enculturations).[1] Different enculturations may mean that younger faculty and/or more recently graduated Ph.Ds may have dissimilar relations to writing and the field of rhetoric and composition. If the value placed on one's literacies is shifting, that knowledge may terrify, anger, or interest, and can mean different relations to the cohort with whom one was enculturated into the field. In addition, people heed calls to disparate life-course trajectories and encounter each other in the midst of their dissonant definitions of what constitutes a life well lived. How we learn in the midst of these challenging terrains needs to be assessed.

Finally, in aging research, we need to determine how race, class, gender, regional location, and so forth, influence the choices people make. As researchers, we have to decide the degree to which we will attempt to understand the challenges people face financially and emotionally that are

---

[1]Although the trend often is for younger people to be enculturated into a field when in their twenties, older students who enter are marked by the time period in which they receive their degree. Thus it make sense to pay attention to both enculturation cohort and age cohort.

often linked to cumulative advantages/disadvantages based on identity categories. In addition, students, peers, and administrators may have expectations that reveal bias and discriminatory attitudes towards age. A researcher must determine how to tap into that information, and a researcher must decide how much attention should be paid to body ability and the risks people take because of their sense of their bodies.

The challenge in this text, then, is to somehow shape a project that understands the existing power structures, probes the individuals' relations to learning, explores the impact of literacy traditions for adult learners, and checks for the important issues surrounding aging. The first three issues (power, individual learning, and literacy traditions) are familiar territory for our field, and we have rich traditions conducting research to explore these concerns. However, we don't have as much experience with aging, and a project shaped around writing faculty would need to consider which aging concerns it wants to explore and what methodologies one will use. In my own work, I keep that image of the rackity bridge in mind and question how to "refuse the acquisitive model of power-knowledge," how to create a relationship in which learning thrives, a pedagogy that Phelan might embrace. I think such a goal requires me to be more cognizant of the multiple issues playing in this situation of faculty development. I have increasingly decided to attempt research that combines quantitative and qualitative research, because we need to see this aging issue in all its complexity.

In order to conduct quantitative research that addresses aging, I look to what other fields have done. This strategy needs to be considered carefully. Peter Mortensen and Gesa Kirsch suggest that we need to examine what it means to import interdisciplinary research methods into our field. Talking specifically about qualitative studies, they say that "there remains a pressing need to scrutinize what it means to import, adapt, select, and transform ethnographic and case study methods in order to investigate literacy and writing communities" (xx). This holds true for quantitative studies as well. Nonetheless, I want to suggest some of the possibilities in aging studies research by describing a recent quantitative study by Sara J. Czaja et al.

To follow the work of Czaja is to watch the major corporations' influence on what we know about older adults and learning computer-based skills. As she and her colleagues have progressed in their methodologies, what we know about how older adults learn has also shifted—though the kinds of tasks and skills studied are particularly mundane. Her studies often focus on training older adults to perform data entry and retrieval tasks, perhaps in order to assess the cost benefits of employing older adults. Czaja doesn't state her reasons in these terms, but I assume that they study tasks designed for an insurance company because a corporation wants to know how older adults perform compared to younger and middle-aged adults and what might improve productivity. In the article "Examining Age Differences in Performance of a Complex Information Search and Retrieval Task," Czaja et al. describe their research design. With a diverse 117 participants, who were paid $125 for five days, five hours a day, with not only young (20–39) and older (60–75) participants but also middle-aged (40–59 years), Czaja et al. conducted a "cognitive battery consisting of 15 tests" that "identify the following abilities: processing speed, visuomotor skills, language and verbal fluency, abstraction, attention, working memory, and long-term storage" (566).

The first day of the study was used for the battery of cognitive tests. The participants were trained on the second day, and procedures were in place to make sure that they were able to understand the material (567). On the third through fifth days, "the participants performed the task on their own for approximately 3 hrs each day" (567) with rest periods and tests. From the statistical analysis, Czaja et al. are able to give some interesting findings. "Overall, the data indicated that although performance improved for all participants with task experience, the older people performed at lower levels than the other participants except for navigational efficiency and conditionalized navigation" (572). Although the older people performed at lower levels, "the data suggested that the older participants may have benefited more than the younger people from task experience. Across the 3 days the difference between the younger and older participants diminished, and only the older participants showed improvement" (574). From this research, they suggest that "for this task individual differences in age, processing speed, memory, and verbal skill are important for initial learning of the task; however, further improvements in performance are largely predicted by practice" (574), particularly for the older participants.

The value of this particular situation is that it "provided an opportunity for examining the influence of basic cognitive abilities on the performance of a real-world task" (572). For example, as the insurance modeled task also involved the ability to answer phones, at designated times, the participant would receive a phone call and would be evaluated on his or her ability to answer the question, simulating the work environment. The next ostensible step in such a study, it would seem, would be to take this actual experiment into the field, but then controlling for variables becomes more of a challenge. These studies often control the environment down to the amount of white noise that a participant experiences, an important issue for older adults because of potential hearing-loss issues.

In discussing the relation of the lab and the real world environment, Neil Charness et al. describe the lab setting as useful for holding "constant as many variables as possible that might be involved in performance, manipulating just the few we feel are critical to the process we are investigating" (221). Although we understand the necessity of this kind of research, Charness et al. admit that "in psychology generally, and in the cognitive aging research in particular, we tend to be weakest in evaluating that part of the scientific cycle that deals with testing our predictions in the world and bringing those results back into the lab for reexamination" (222). The challenge and conundrum of research includes holding the variables steady enough to manipulate the ones that are believed to determine behavior, given the "real world" environments in which actual behavior occurs.

Many aging studies approach questions from a quantitative perspective, and I think a researcher decides, based on the questions to be answered, the necessity of a quantitative study. The research also needs to address the intended audience. As Cindy Johanek has so eloquently pointed out, ours is a field that tends to favor qualitative research. I agree with Johanek's assessment that we are reluctant to embrace quantitative studies, and I think aging work in our field should combine qualitative and quantitative research, not only to address viable questions and to meet our discipline and interdisciplinary audience expectations, but also to have as full a range of awareness as possible as we try to develop curriculum.

I imagine a study focused on under or over-accommodation in curriculum materials. Faculty could be observed and timed, working individually with a trainer who kept to a script, and we could measure efficacy in accommodation. Once I had the results from this research, I could test for negative and positive stereotyping by embedding images into on-screen training and could determine what kinds of effects such priming had on faculty members' abilities to learn. With curriculum information and priming findings in hand, we could move to tests that assess student bias regarding older teachers in the classroom by scripting interactions between older faculty and students in order to assess the communication strategies of students. In addition, faculty could report on how they experienced students' communications. Sequences could be determined and viable expectations could be established for how long it might take for a faculty member to learn multiple programs. At more systemic levels, we could develop questionnaires to distribute across the nation to a representative sample of first-year writing programs. Such data would help us to understand the available resources and structures that are used for training.

These are legitimate ways of imagining research that tries to assess faculty training. We have the possibility of breaking down parts of the process of teaching and determining the degree to which we integrate the methodologies from other fields. In addition, future research needs to recognize that the study of writing faculty in terms of technology training remains a politically charged situation. To study faculty development is to enter the quagmire of local funding decisions. On any campus, one can determine how the resources are being distributed, and research would need to assess the efficacy of current practices. In addition, investigations into a university's current practices regarding technology training may reveal the values placed on changing technologies. Such studies also reveal current practices for rewarding new learning and suggest existing power structures. Finally, a look at actual training can reveal how the existing structure benefits some populations and disadvantages others. To recommend shifts in current practice is to disrupt the existing power dynamics at a range of levels.

These local political realities are then merged with the nature of instruction when considering research methods. To study learning of this type is to study classrooms, and we have many traditions of studying students in literacy training situations.

In my initial work with faculty training research, I've drawn on these traditions, using long interviews, focus groups, and questionnaires. From the work Suellynn Duffey and I have completed, I know that I'm interested in creating learning communities of peer age faculty, and I want to test the role that the research itself plays in the pedagogical framework. We discovered in the research that we've already done that the questions we were raising contributed to people's perceptions. The process itself of thinking through what had happened in training sessions eased the anxiety people felt, and the paradigm of a research project gave us a clear sense of the material they would try to learn and provided a venue in which they could discuss their anxieties. Yeatts et al. suggest that pedagogy should overview how inclusion of technologies will affect teachers. They speak of policy changes, but their wording is useful for this work. Teachers need a "detailed and carefully presented account of just what changes will be made and their anticipated effects on the individual employees and the organization as a whole" (573). But they also indicate that people need to "learn at their own pace" with "their age peers" and that people function better when their "anxieties associated with learning something new are addressed" (575). I anticipate future projects that will try to understand what is happening at two levels. First, the kind of work that Yeatts et al. describe will be pursued, and second, curriculum materials will be assessed, along with stereotyping and other tests. If we combine quantitative and qualitative research, particularly examining the possibilities of a rackety bridge metaphor, I think there's the opportunity to create better working conditions for our faculty.

FAILED CONVERSIONS AND FURTHER RESEARCH

Today, as I was trying to figure a way to finish up this conclusion, I found myself writing "what if they don't convert?" What if the faculty decide that literacy accumulation, is not worth their time or investment? A viable question. Well, it's not my job to convert, I think immediately. However I also I think that I'd lose out as a result. I would lose the possibility of community, of people with perspectives other than my own, perspectives that I know would push me to think differently about the values I hold. But I'm not evangelical, I don't think. Raised with that zeal, yes, but ambivalent about those proclivities as an adult. I won't go door to door. All I seem to be interested in is eliminating certain barriers that stand in the way of people's abilities to learn. If thoughtfully done, we might allow people more of a possibility to feel like they have a choice in what they learn. That's as far as my zeal carries me, I hope.

I chose to look intensely at faculty development for this discussion on aging literacies, but I want to conclude by talking about other research that I find equally as intriguing and that suggests other routes and possibilities for this kind of work.

Technical And Professional Writing—
How to Write Readable Text

In my research with technical and professional writing, I'm hoping to look at what makes web sites readable for older adults and what effect constraints (sites friendly for seniors) have on design considerations, so that we can better provide instruction to writing students when they write for an increasingly aging population of readers. We need to know how to teach students to write more effective prose for elder populations. There are multiple issues at stake for technical and professional writing. When students learn the communication issues older adults face, they can begin to understand how and why fraud happens. Whether it's a butterfly ballot in Florida or the questions raised about Publisher's Clearing House marketing methods, older adults may be vulnerable to certain kinds of misreadings. To show students the ethical issues involved in communicating with older adults is to prepare them for the workplace.

Health Literacies (a Variety of Venues)

When our field examines health literacy material, from a variety of angles, we should find the question of age to be a significant one. In other research, I've begun investigating rhetorics on women's health, particularly examining the rhetorical strategies used for women of different races. Although some books are specifically about aging (e.g., Christiane Northrup's *The Wisdom of Menopause*), others are more generally dealing with women's health. This kind of work has multiple directions—from usability studies and professional writing to more personal writing on the impact of such rhetorics on a woman's life.

On-Line Communities

Disparate opportunities exist on-line for older adults based on their placement within the society. For example, Senior Net is focused more on issues relevant to middle-class older adults whereas Green Thumb seems to be designed for older, poorer adults seeking further employment in old age. I continue to study the strategies older adults use in personal ads on-line, and I find the on-line communities for people in general to be interesting places to conduct research. When people participate on sites that are designed for them based on age—the information/discussions/research that is available at these sites is quite intriguing. The possibility for comparing real life local scenes for older adults with these virtual life on-line communities would provide more information about how community works. Older adults are increasingly accessing the web to look for information on health, and a variety of other issues. Because the on-line searches are always increasing in complexity, and because programs are always going to change, I think there's some possibility for extended studies of strategies individuals bring to the process of accumulating WWW kinds of literacies.

* * *

The possibilities for research regarding aging are numerous. Almost every subdiscipline in our field could create studies that integrate aging issues into research designs. Although this book has focused on one example—

faculty development and workplace literacies—a focus that is of interest to literacy studies, writing program administration, and professional workplace writing, I hope that the book gives directions to researchers in other areas who might be able to take up aging in their research, whether they study assessment or coordinate writing centers. The possibilities exist to integrate aging concerns into our studies, and clearly we need to address aging, particularly when intertwined with other identities, because age plays a role in our findings whether we address it or not. Our field needs to consider aging issues with the same sophistication with which we address gender, race, class, region, body ability, orientation, and religious affiliations.

REFERENCES

"Age Data" U.S. Census Bureau. http://www.census.gov/population/www/socde-mo/age.html (accessed June 1, 2004).

Althusser, Louis "Ideology and Ideological State Apparatuses" *Lenin and Philosophy, and Other Essays*. Ed. London: New Left Books, 1971. 136–170.

Baddeley, Alan. "The Concept of Working Memory: A View of its Current State and Probable Future Development." *Cognition* 10 (1981): 17–23.

Baddeley, Alan D. and Robert H. Logie. "Working Memory: The Multiple-Component Model." *Models of Working Memory: Mechanisms of Active Maintenance and Executive Control*. Eds. Akira Miyake and Priti Shah. Cambridge: Cambridge UP, 1999. 28–62.

Balatti, Jo and Ian Falk. "Socioeconomic Contributions of Adult Learning to Community: A Social Capital Perspective. *Adult Education Quarterly* 52.4 (August 2002): 281–298.

Bargh, John A., March Chen, and Lara Burrows. "Automaticity of Social Behavior: Direct Effects of Trait Construct and Stereotype Activation on Action." *Journal of Personality and Social Psychology* 71.2 (1996): 230-244.

Barker, Thomas T. and Fred Kemp. "Network Theory: A Postmodern Pedagogy for the Writing Classroom." *Computers and Community*. Ed. Carolyn Handa. Portsmouth: Boynton/Cook, 1990. 1–27.

Bartholomae, David. "Inventing the University." *Journal of Basic Writing* 5 (1986): 4–23.

Barton, Ellen. "Interpreting the Discourses of Technology." *Literacy and Computers: The Complications of Teaching and Learning with Technology*. Eds. Cynthia L. Selfe and Susan Hilligoss. New York: MLA, 1994. 56–75.

Bateson, Mary Catherine. *Peripheral Visions: Learning Along the Way.* New York: Harper Perennial, 1995. Reissue edition.

Bauman, Zygmunt. *Mortality, Immortality, and Other Life Strategies.* Stanford: Stanford UP, 1992.

Bennett, E and Susan Eklund, "Vision Changes, Intelligence, and Aging: Parts I & II." *Educational Gerontology* 9 (1983): 255–278; 435–442.

Bikson, Karra L. and Tora K. Bikson. "The Impact of Internet Use Over Time on Older Adults: A Field Experiment." *Communication, Technology and Aging: Opportunities and Challenges for the Future.* Eds. Neil Charness, Denise C. Parks and Bernhard A. Sabel. New York: Springer, 2001. 127–149.

Biggs, Simon. *The Mature Imagination: Dynamics of Identity in Midlife and Beyond.* Buckingham: Open UP, 1999.

Billett, Stephen. "Toward a Workplace Pedagogy: Guidance, Participation, and Engagement." *Adult Education Quarterly* 53.1 (Nov. 2002): 27–43.

Blaikie, Andrew. *Aging and Popular Culture.* Cambridge: Cambridge UP, 1999.

Botwinick, Jack, & Martha Storandt. *Memory, Relation Function and Age.* Springfield, IL: Charles C. Thomas, 1974.

Braithwaite, Valerie. "Reducing Ageism." *Ageism: Stereotyping and Prejudice Against Older Persons.* Ed. Todd D. Nelson. Cambridge: MIT, 2002. 312–337.

Brandt, Deborah. "Accumulating Literacies." *College English* 576 (1995): 649–667.

Brodkey, Linda. *Writing Permitted in Designated Areas Only.* Minneapolis: U of Minnesota P, 1996.

Browne, Colette V. *Women, Feminism and Aging.* New York: Springer, 1998.

Bruffee, Kenneth A. "Collaborative Learning and the Conversation of Mankind." *College English* 46.7 (1984): 635–652.

Burke, Deborah M. "Language Production and Aging." *Constraints on Language: Aging, Grammar, and Memory.* Eds. Susan Kemper, and Reinhold Kliegl. Boston: Kluwer, 1999. 3–28.

Butler, Judith. *Gender Trouble.* New York: Routledge, 1990.

Butler, Judith. *Bodies that Matter: On the Discursive Limits of "Sex".* New York: Routledge, 1993.

Carp, Frances M. "Living Arrangements for Midlife and Older Women." *Handbook on Women and Aging.* Ed. Jean M. Coyle. Westport: Greenwood P, 1997. 112–128.

Charness, Neil, and Elizabeth A. Bosman, "Human Factors and Aging." *Handbook of Aging and Cognition.* Eds. F.I.M. Craik and T. A. Salthouse. Hillsdale, NJ: Erlbaum, 1992. 595–545.

Charness, Neil, Elizabeth Bosman, Catherine Kelley, and Melvin Mottram. "Cognitive Theory and Word Processing Training: When Prediction Fails." *Aging and Skilled Performance.* Eds. Wendy A. Rogers, Arthur D. Fisk, and Neff Walker. Mahwah, NJ: Erlbaum, 1996, 221–239.

Charney, Davida. "The Effect of Hypertext on Processes of Reading and Writing." *Literacy and Computers: The Complications of Teaching and Learning with Technology.* New York: Modern Language Association, 1994. 238–263.

Conway-Turner, Kate. "Older Women of Color: A Feminist Exploration of the Intersections of Personal, Familial and Community Life." *Fundamentals of Feminist Gerontology.* Ed. J. Dianne Garner. Binghampton, NY: Haworth, 1999. 115–130.

Cope, Bill and Mary Kalantzis. Eds. *Multiliteracies: Literacy Learning and the Design of Social Futures.* New York: Routledge, 2000.

Cornell, Drucilla. *At the Heart of Freedom.* Princeton, NJ: Princeton UP, 1998.

Craik, Fergus I. M., and T. A. Salthouse. (2000). *The Handbook of Aging and Cognition.* Mahwah, NJ: Erlbaum.

Crow, Angela. "Computers and Aging: Marking Raced, Classed, and Gendered Inequalities." *Journal of Technical Writing and Communication* 32.1 (2002): 23–44.

————. "What's Age Got to Do with it?: Teaching Older Students in Computer-Aided Classrooms." *Teaching English in the Two Year College* 27.4 (May 2000): 400–406.

Cristofovici, Anca. "Touching Surfaces: Photography, Aging and an Aesthetics of Change." *Figuring Age: Women, Bodies, Generations.* Ed. Kathleen Woodward. Bloomington: Indiana UP, 1999. 268–293.

Cruikshank, Margaret. *Learning to Be Old: Gender, Culture and Aging.* Lanham: Rowman, 2003.

Cuddy, Amy J. C. and Susan T. Fiske. "Doddering but Dear: Process, Content, and Function in Stereotyping of Older Persons." *Ageism: Stereotyping Prejudice Against Older Persons.* Ed. Todd D. Nelson. Cambridge: MIT, 2002. 3–26.

Cushman, Ellen. *The Struggle and The Tools: Oral and Literate Strategies in an Inner City Community.* Albany: SUNY Press, 1998.

————. "Multimedia Compositions and Their Challenge to Visual Literacy and Rhetoric." Conference on College Composition and Communication. Chicago, IL, March 2002.

Cutler, Stephen J. and Jon Hendricks. "Emerging Social Trends." *Handbook of Aging and the Social Sciences.* Eds. Robert H. Binstock and Linda K. George. 5th edition. San Diego: Academic P, 2001. 462–480.

Czaja, Sara J., Joseph Sharit, Raymond Ownby, David L. Roth, and Sankaran Nair. "Examining Age Differences in Performance of a Complex Information Search and Retrieval Task." *Psychology and Aging* 16.4 (2001): 564–579.

Czaja, Sara J., Joseph Sharit, Sankara Nair, & Mark Rubert. (1998). "Understanding Sources of User Variability in Computer-Based Data Entry Performance." *Behaviour & Information Technology* 17(1998): 282–293.

Daley, Barbara J. "Learning and Professional Practice: A Study of Four Professions." *Adult Education Quarterly* 52.1 (Nov. 2001): 39–54.

Daneman, Meredyth and Twila Tardif. "Working Memory and Reading Skill Re-examined." *Attention and Performance XII: The Psychology of Reading.* Ed. M. Coltheart. Hillsdale: Erlbaum, 1987. 491–508.

Davey, Judith A. "Active Ageing and Education in Mid and later Life. *Aging and Society* 22 (2002): 95–113.

DiPardo, Anne. *A Kind of Passport: A Basic Writing Adjunct Program and the Challenge of Diversity.* Urbana, IL: NCTE, 1993.

Direct Effects of Trait Construct and Stereotype Activation on Action." *Journal of Personality and Social Psychology* 71.2 (1996): 230–244.

Dobrin, David N. "Second Response: Hype and Hypertext." *Literacy and Computers: The Complications of Teaching and Learning with Technology.* Eds. Cynthia L. Selfe and Susan Hilligoss. New York: MLA 1994. 305–318.

Dunn, Patricia. *Learning Re-abled.* Portsmouth, NH: Boyton/Cook, 1995.

Dweck, Carol S. "Motivational Processes Affecting Learning." *American Psychologist* 41.10 (October 1986): 1040–1048.

Echt, K. V. "Designing Web-Based Health Information for Older Adults: Visual Considerations and Design Directives." *Older Adults, Health Information, and the World Wide Web.* Ed. R. W. Morrell. Mahwah, NJ: Erlbaum, 2002. 61–88.

Edwards, Richard, and Robin Usher. "Lifelong Learning: A Postmodern Condition of Education?" *Adult Education Quarterly* 51.4 (Aug 2001) 273–287.

Edwards, Richard, Julia Clarke, Roger Harrison and Fiona Reeve. "Is There Madness in the Method? Representations of Research in Lifelong Learning." *Adult Education Quarterly* 52.2 (Feb. 2002): 128–139.

Eldred, Janet Carey. "The Technology of Voice." *College Composition & Communication* 48.3 (1997): 334–347.

Enos, Theresa. *Gender Roles and Faculty Lives in Rhetoric and Composition.* Carbondale: Southern Illinois UP, 1997.

Erikson, Erik H. *Childhood and Society.* 2nd Ed. New York: Norton, 1963.

Facio, Elisa. "Chicanas and Aging: Toward Definitions of Womanhood." *Handbook on Women and Aging.* Ed. Jean M. Coyle. Westport, CT: Greenwood P, 1997. 335–350.

Faigley, Lester. "Beyond Imagination: The Internet and Global Digital Literacy." *Passions, Pedagogies and 21st Century Technologies.* Eds. Gail E. Hawisher and Cynthia L. Selfe. Logan: Utah UP, 1999.

Farr, Marcia. "Essayist Literacy and Other Verbal Performances." *Written Communication* 10:1 (1993): 4-38.

Featherstone, Mike. "Post-Bodies, Aging and Virtual Reality." *Images of Ageing: Cultural Representations of Later Life.* Ed. Mike Featherstone and Andrew Wernick. London: Routledge, 1995. 227–243.

Featherstone, Mike and Mike Hepworth. "Images of Positive Aging: A Case Study of *Retirement Choice* Magazine." *Images of Ageing: Cultural Representations of Later Life.* Ed. Mike Featherstone and Andrew Wernick. London: Routledge, 1995. 29–60.

Felman, Shoshana. *Jacques Lacan and the Adventure of Insight: Psychoanalysis in Contemporary Culture.* Cambridge: Harvard UP, 1989.

Ferraro, Kenneth F. "Aging and Role Transitions." *Handbook of Aging and the Social Sciences.* Eds. Robert H. Binstock and Linda K. George. 5th edition. San Diego: Academic P, 2001. 313–329.

Foucault, Michel. *The History of Sexuality: Volume I: An Introduction.* New York: Vintage Random House, 1980. Translated by Robert Hurley.

Fox, Tom. *Defending Access: A Critique of Standards in Higher Education.* Portsmouth: Boynton/Cook Heinemann, 1999.

Freire, Paulo. *Pedagogy of the Oppressed.* New York: Continuum, 1989. Translated by Myra Bergman Ramos.

George, Diana and Shoos. "Response: Dropping Bread Crumbs in the Intertextual Forest: Critical Literacy in a Postmodern Age." *Passions and Pedagogies and 21st Century Technologies.* Eds. Gail E. Hawisher and Cynthia L. Selfe. Logan: Utah UP, 1999.

Gernsbacher, Morton Ann and Mark E. Faust. "The Mechanism of Suppression: A Component of General Comprehension Skill." *Journal of Experimental Psychology: Learning, Memory, and Cognition* 17.2 (1991): 245–262.

Gilyard, Keith. *Voices of the Self: A Study of Language Competence.* Detroit: Wayne State UP, 1991.

Gordimer, Nadine. *Burger's Daughter.* London: Penguin, 1979.

Graham, Joseph F. Ed. *Difference in Translation.* Ithaca, NY: Cornell UP, 1985.

Greenberg, Jeff, Jeff Schimel, and Andy Mertens. "Ageism: Denying the Face of the Future." *Ageism: Stereotyping and Prejudice against Older Persons.* Ed. Todd D. Nelson. Cambridge, MA: MIT, 2002. 27–48.

Grigar, Dene, Annie Olson, Susie Crowson, Pat Nolan, Carl Clark, and Cecie Huddleston. "Introducing TWUMOO: Cyberspaces for Teaching, Learning, and Research." The Second Biennial Feminism(s) and Rhetoric(s) Conference, October 1999, Minneapolis, MN.

Gullette, Margaret Morganroth. "Age Studies as Cultural Studies" *Handbook of Humanities and Aging.* Eds. Thomas R. Cole, Robert Kastenbaum, and Ruth E. Ray. 2nd ed. 214–234.

Haas, Christina and Christine M. Neuwirth. *Literacy and Computers: The Complications Of Teaching and Learning with Technology.* Eds. Cynthia L. Selfe and Susan Hilligoss. NY: MLA, 1994 319–335.

Hagestad, Gunhild O. and Dale Dannefer. "Concepts and Theories of Aging: Beyond Microfication in Social Science Approaches." *Handbook of Aging and the Social Sciences.* Eds. Robert H. Binstock and Linda K. George. 5th ed. San Diego: Academic P, 2001. 3–21.

Handa, Carolyn. "Politics, Ideology, and the Strange, Slow Death of the Isolated Composer or Why We Need Community in the Writing Classroom." *Computers and Community.* Portsmouth: Boynton/Cook, 1990. 160–184.

Haraven, Tamara K. "Historical Perspectives on Aging and Family Relations." *Handbook of Aging and the Social Sciences.* Eds. Robert H. Binstock and Linda K. George. 5th ed. San Diego: Academic P, 2001. 141–159.

Haraway, Donna J. Modest_Witness@Second_Millenium. *femaleMan_Meets_Oncomouse.* New York: Routledge, 1997.

Hartley, Joellen T. "Aging and Prose Memory: Tests of the Resource-Deficit Hypothesis." *Psychology and Aging* 8.4 (1993): 538–551.

Hartley, Joellen T. et al. "Reading Speed and Prose Memory in Older and Younger Adults." *Psychology and Aging* 9.2 (1994): 216–223.

Hausdorff, Jeffrey M., Becca R. Levy, and Jeanne Y. Wei. "The Power of Ageism on Physical Function of Older Persons: Reversibility of Age-Related Gait Changes." *Journal of American Geriatrics Society* 47 (1999): 1346–1349.

Hawisher, Gail E. and Paul LeBlanc. Eds. *Re-Imagining Computers and Composition: Teaching and Research in the Virtual Age.* Portsmouth, NH: Boynton/Cook, 1992.

Hawisher, Gail E. and Cynthia L. Selfe. Eds. *Passions, Pedagogies and 21st Century Technologies.* Logan: Utah State UP, 1999.

Hawisher, Gail and Patricia A. Sullivan. "Fleeting Images: Women Visually Writing the Web." *Passions, Pedagogies and 21st Century Technologies.* Eds. Gail E. Hawisher and Cynthia L. Selfe. Logan: Utah State UP, 1999.

Hayes, John R. "A New Framework for Understanding Cognition and Affect in Writing." Reprinted in *Literacy: A Critical Sourcebook.* Eds. Ellen Cushman, Eugene R. Kintgen, Barry M. Kroll, and Mike Rose. Boston: Bedford St. Martin: 2001. 172–198. Originally in *The Science of Writing* eds. C. Michael Levy and Sarah Ransdell. Mahwah, NY: Erlbaum, 1996. 1–27.

Heath, Shirley Brice. *Ways with Words. Language, Life and Work in Communities and Classrooms.* Cambridge, MA: Harvard UP, 1983.

Helson, Ravenna. "The Self in Middle Age." *Multiple Paths of Midlife Development.* Eds. Margie E. Lachman and Jacquelyn Boone James. Chicago: U of Chicago P, 1997. 21–43.

Henretta, John C. "Work and Retirement." *Handbook of Aging and the Social Sciences.* Eds. Robert H. Binstock and Linda K. George. 5th ed. San Diego: Academic P, 2001. 255–271.

Hiatt, Lorraine G. "Designing for the Vision and Hearing Impairments of the Elderly." *Housing the Aged.* Eds. Victor Regnier and John Pynoos. New York: Elsevier. 341–371.

Hockey, Jenny and Allison James. *Growing up and Growing Old: Ageing and Dependency in the Life Course.* London, Sage: 1993.

Holt, Barbara J. and Roger W. Morrell. "Guidelines for Web Site Design for Older Adults: The Ultimate Influence of Cognitive Factors." *Older Adults, Health Information, and the World Wide Web.* Ed. Roger Morrell. Mahwah: Erlbaum, 2002. 109–129.

Horner, Bruce and Min-Zhan Lu. *Representing the "Other": Basic Writers and the Teaching of Basic Writing.* Urbana, IL: NCTE, 1999.

Howell, Sharon L., Vicki K. Carter, and Fred M. Schied. "Gender and Women's Experience at Work: A Critical and Feminist Perspective on Human Resource Development." *Adult Education Quarterly* 52.2 (Feb. 2002): 112–127.

Hoyer, William J., George W. Rebok, and Marx Sved. "Effects of Varying Irrelevant Information on Adult Age Differences in Problem Solving." *Journal of Gerontology* 34(1979): 553–560.

Hummert, Mary Lee, John M. Wiemann, and Jon F. Nussbaum. Eds. *Interpersonal Communication in Older Adulthood: Interdisciplinary Theory and Research.* Thousand Oaks, CA: Sage, 1994.

Hummert, Mary Lee, Teri A Garstka, Laurie, T. O'Brien, Anthony G. Greenwald, and Deborah S. Mellott. "Using the Implicit Association Test to Measure Age Differences in Implicit Social Cognitions." *Psychology and Aging* 17.3 (2002): 482–495.

Hummert, Mary Lee, Teri A. Garstka, Jaye L. Shaner, and Sharon Strahm. "Stereotypes of the Elderly Held by Young, Middle-Aged, and Elderly Adults." *Journal of Gerontology* 49.4 (Sept. 1994): 240–249.

Hummert, Mary Lee, Jaye L. Shaner, Teri A. Garstka, and Clark Henry. "Communication with Older Adults: The Influence of Age Stereotypes, Context, and Communicator Age." *Human Communication Research* 25.1 (Sept. 1998): 124–151.

Johanek, Cindy. *Composing Research: A Contextualist Research Paradigm for Rhetoric and Composition.* Logan: Utah State UP, 2000.

Johnson-Eilola, Johndan. *Nostalgic Angels: Rearticulating Hypertext Writing.* Greenwich, CT: Ablex/Greenwood Press, 1997.

Jones, Gill. "Marriage Partners and Their Class Trajectories." *The Social Mobility of Women: Beyond Male Mobility Models.* Eds. Geoff Payne and Pamela Abbott. Bristol: Falmer, 1990. 101–119.

Just, Marcel Adam and Patricia A. Carpenter. "A Capacity Theory of Comprehension: Individual Differences in Working Memory." *Psychological Review* 99.1 (1992): 122–149.

Kaplan, Nancy. "Ideology, Technology, and the Future of Writing Instruction." *Evolving Perspectives on Computers and Composition Studies: Questions for the 1990s.* Eds Gail Hawisher and Cynthia L. Selfe. Urbana: NCTE and *Computers and Composition,* 1991. 11–42.

Katz Stephen. "Imagining the Life-span: From Premodern Miracles to Postmodern Fantasies." *Images of Ageing: Cultural Representations of Later Life.* Eds. Mike Featherstone and Andrew Wernick. London: Routledge, 1995. 61–75.

Kaufman, Gayle and Glen H. Elder, Jr. "Revisiting Age Identity: A Research Note." *Journal of Aging Studies* 16 (2002): 169–176.

Kemper, Susan. "Over-Accommodations and Under-Accommodations to Aging." *Communication, Technology and Aging: Opportunities and Challenges for the Future.* Eds. Neil Charness, Denise C. Parks, and Bernhard A. Sabel. New York: Springer, 2001. 30–46.

Kingsolver, Barbara. *The Poisonwood Bible: A Novel.* New York: Perennial, 1999.

Kirsch, Gesa E. *Women Writing the Academy: Audience, Authority, and Transformation. Studies in Writing and Rhetoric.* Carbondale: Southern Illinois UP, 1992.

Kite, Mary E. and Lisa Smith Wagner. "Attitudes Towards Older Adults." *Ageism: Stereotyping and Prejudice Against Older Persons.* Ed. Todd D. Nelson. Cambridge, MA: MIT, 2002. 129–161.

Kress, Gunter. "'English' at the Crossroads: Rethinking Curricula of Communication in the Context of the Turn to the Visual." *Passions, Pedagogies and 21st Century Technologies.* Eds. Gail E. Hawisher and Cynthia L. Selfe. Logan: Utah State UP, 1999. 66–88.

_____."Multimodality" *Multiliteracies: Literacy Learning and the Design of Social Futures.* Eds. Bill Cope and Mary Kalantzis. New York: Routledge, 2000. 182–202.

Kressley, Konrad M. and Mark Huebschmann "The 21st Century Campus: Gerontological Perspectives." *Educational Gerontology* 28(2002): 835-851.

Lachman, Margie E. and Jacquelyn Boone James. "Charting the Course of Midlife Development: An Overview." *Multiple Pathes of Midlife Development.* Eds. Margie E. Lachman and Jacquelyn Boone James. Chicago: U of Chicago P, 1997. 1–17.

Laslett, Peter. *A Fresh Map of Life: Emergence of the Third Age.* London: Orion, 1989.

Laubach Training Methods. http://www.open.org/ ~ literacy/laubach.htm (accessed may 24, 2004).

Lawrence, David. "The 1999 MLA Survey of Staffing in English and Foreign Language Departments." *Profession* 2001. Available on-line. http://www.mla.org/pdf/staffing_survey.pdf (accessed June 1, 2004).

Lemke, J. L. "Metamedia Literacy: Transforming Meanings and Media." http://academic.brooklyn.cuny.edu/education/jlemke/reinking.htm (accessed May 24, 2004) in *Handbook of Literacy and Technology: Transformations in a Post-Typographic World.* Ed. David Reinking. Mahwah, NJ: Erlbaum, 1998.

Levy, Becca, R. and Mahzarin R. Banaji. "Implicit Ageism." *Ageism: Stereotyping and Prejudice against Older Persons.* Ed. Todd D. Nelson. Cambridge, MA: MIT, 2002. 49–75.

Levy, Becca R., Jeffery M. Hausdorff, Rebecca Hencke, and Jeanne Y. Wei. "Reducing Cardiovascular Stress with Positive Self-Stereotypes of Aging." *The Journals of Gerontology* 55B.4 (July 2000): 205–213.

Lindemann, Erika with Daniel Anderson. *A Rhetoric for Writing Teachers.* 4th Ed. New York: Oxford UP, 2001.

Lohman, Margaret C. "Environmental Inhibitors to Informal Learning in the Workplace: A Case Study of Public School Teachers." *Adult Education Quarterly* 50.2 (feb. 2000): 83–101.

Lorde, Audre. *Sister Outsider: Essays & Speeches.* Freedom, CA: Crossing P, 1984.

Luke, Carmen. "Cyber-Schooling and Technological Change: Multiliteracies for New Times." *Multiliteracies: Literacy Learning and the Design of Social Futures.* Ed Bill Cope and Mary Kalantzis. New York: Routledge, 2000. 69–91.

Lunsford, Andrea A. and Lisa Ede. "Rhetoric in a New Key: Women and Collaboration." *Rhetoric Review* 8.2 (1990): 234–241.

Malinowitz, Harriet. *Textual Orientations: Lesbian and Gay Students and the Making of Discourse Communities.* Portsmouth, NH: Heinemann, 1995.

Markson, Elizabeth W. "Sagacious, Sinful, or Superfluous? The Social Construction of Older Women." *Handbook on Women and Aging.* Ed. Jean M. Coyle. Westport, CT: Greenwood P, 1997. 53–71.

Maso, Carole. "Rupture, Verge, and Precipice / Precipice, Verge, and Hurt Not." *Break Every Rule: Essays on Language, Longing & Moments of Desire.* Washington, DC: Counterpoint, 2000. 161–191.

McCann, Robert and Howard Giles. "Ageism in the Workplace: A Communication Perspective." *Ageism: Stereotyping and Prejudice against Older Persons.* Ed. Todd D. Nelson. Cambridge: MIT, 2002. 163–199.

Mead, Sherry E., Nina Lamson, and Wendy A. Rogers. "Human Factors Guidelines for Web Site Usability: Health-Oriented Web Sites for Older Adults." *Older Adults, Health Information, and the World Wide Web.* Ed. Roger Morrell. Mahwah: Erlbaum, 2002. 89–107.

Meyer, Bonnie, Andrew Talbot, Leonard Poon, Delores Puskar and R. Allen Stubblefield. (1996, April). "Task and Text Factors Differentially Affect the Use of a Reading Strategy by Young and Old Adults." Paper presented at The Cognitive Aging Conference. Atlanta, GA, April 1996.

Miller, Susan. *Textual Carnivals: The Politics of Composition.* Carbondale: Southern Illinois UP, 1991.

Miyake, Akira and Priti Shah. *Models of Working Memory: Mechanisms of Active Maintenance and Executive Control.* Cambridge, England: Cambridge UP, 1999.

Moen, Phyllis. "The Gendered Life Course." *Handbook of Aging and the Social Sciences.* Eds Robert H. Binstock and Linda K. George. 5th Ed. San Diego: Academic P, 2001. 179–196.

Montepare, Joann M. and Leslie A. Zebrowitz. "A Social-Developmental View of Ageism." *Ageism: Stereotyping and Prejudice against Older Persons.* Ed. Todd D. Nelson. Cambridge, MA: MIT, 2002. 77–125.

Moran, Charles. "Access: The A-Word in Technology Studies." *Passions, Pedagogies and 21st Century Technologies.* Eds. Gail E. Hawisher and Cynthia L. Selfe. Logan: Utah State UP, 1999. 205–220.

Morrell, Carolyn M. "Empowerment and Long-Living Women: Return to the Rejected Body." *Journal of Aging Studies* 17(2003) 69–85.

Morrell, Roger. Ed. *Older Adults, Health Information, and the World Wide Web.* Mahwah, NJ: Erlbaum, 2002.

Morrell, Roger W., Steven R. Dailey, and Katherine V. Echt. "Older Adults and Online Information." Paper presented at the Annual Meeting of the Gerontological Society of America, November, Washington, DC 2000.

Morrell, Roger W. and Kathreine V. Echt. "Instructional Design for Older Computer Users: The Influence of Cognitive Factors." *Aging and Skilled Performances: Advances in Theory and Application.* Eds. Wendy A. Rogers, Arthur D. Fisk, and Neff Walker. Mahwah, NJ: Erlbaum, 1996. 241–265.

Morrell, Roger W. and Katherine V. Echt. "Designing Instructions for Computer Use by Older Adults." *Handbook of Human Factors and the Older Adult.* Eds. A. D. Fisk and W. A. Rogers. New York: Academic Press, 1997. 335–361.

Morrow, Daniel G. and Van O. Leirer. "Designing Medication Instructions for Older Adults." *Processing of Medical Information in Aging Patients.* Eds. D. C. Park, Roger W. Morrell, and K. Shifren. Mahwah, NJ: Erlbaum, 1999. 249–266.

Mortensen, Peter. "Reading Material." *Written Communication* 18 (2001): 395–439.

————. "Figuring Illiteracy: Rustic Bodies and Unlettered Minds in Rural America." *Rhetorical Bodies.* Eds. Jack Selzer and Sharon Crowley. Madison: U of Wisconsin P, 1999. 143–170.

Mortensen, Peter and Gesa E. Kirsch. Eds. *Ethics & Representation*. Urbana: NCTE, 1996.

Nelson, Carey. Ed. *Will Teach for Food: Academic Labor in Crisis*. Minneapolis: U of Minnesota P, 1997.

Nielsen, Jakob. "Usability Testing." *Handbook of Human Factors and Ergonomics*. Ed. Gavriel Salvendy. New York: Wiley, 1997.

Nielsen, J. *Designing Web Usability: The Practice of Simplicity*. Indianapolis: New Riders Publishing, 1999.

Northrup, Christiane. *The Wisdom of Menopause: Creating Physical and Emotional Health and Healing During the Change*. New York: Bantam, 2001.

O'Neill, Peggy and Ellen Schendell. "Locating Writing Programs in Research Universities." *A Field of Dreams: Independent Writing Programs and the Future of Composition Studies*. Eds. Peggy O'Neill, Angela Crow, and Larry Burton. Logan: Utah State UP, 2002.

O'Rand, Angela M. "Stratification and the Life Course: The Forms of Life-Course Capital and Their Interrelationships." *Handbook of Aging and the Social Sciences*. Eds. Robert H. Binstock and Linda K. George. 5th edition. San Diego: Academic P, 2001. 197–213.

Palmore, Erdman B. "Sexism and Ageism." *Handbook of Women and Aging*. Ed. Jean M. Coyle. Westport, CT: Greenwood P, 1997.

Park, Denise C. (1992), "Applied Cognitive Aging Research." *Handbook of Cognition and Aging*. Eds. Fergus I. M. Craik & Timothy A. Salthouse. Mahwah, NJ: Erlbaum, 1992. 449–493.

Parker, Rebecca A. and Carolyn M. Aldwin. "Do Aspects of Gender Identity Change from Early to Middle Adulthood? Disentangling Age, Cohort, and Period Effects." *Multiple Paths of Midlife Development*. Eds. Margie E. Lachman and Jacquelyn Boone James. Chicago: U of Chicago P, 1997. 67–107.

Phelan, Peggy. *Unmarked: The Politics of Performance*. New York: Routledge, 1993.

Poell, Rob F., Ferd J. VanDerKrogt, and John H. M. Warmerdam. "Project-Based Learning in Professional Organizations." *Adult Education Quarterly* 49.1 (Fall 1998): 28–42.

Ray, Ruth E. "The Uninvited Guest: Mother/Daughter Conflict in Feminist Gerontology." *Journal of Aging Studies* 17 (2003): 113–128.

Rife, John C. "Middle-Aged and Older Women in the Work Force." *Handbook of Women and Aging*. Ed. Jean M. Coyle. Westport, CT: Greenwood P, 1997.

Richardson, Virgina E. "Women and Retirement." *Fundamentals of Feminist Gerontology*. Ed. J. Dianne Garner. Binghamton, NY: Haworth P, 1999. 49–66.

Rife, John C. "Middle-Aged and Older Women in the Work Force." *Handbook on Women and Aging*. Ed. Jean M. Coyle. Westport, CT: Greenwood P, 1997. 93–111.

Riviere, Cameron N., and Natish V. Thakor. "Effects of Age and Disability on Tracking Tasks with a Computer Mouse: Accuracy and linearity." *Journal of Rehabilitation Research and Development*, 33(1996) 6–15.

Rogers, Wendy A., and Arthur D. Fisk. "Human Factors, Applied Cognition, and Aging." *The Handbook of Aging and Cognition.* Eds. Fergus I.M. Craik and Timothy A. Salthouse. 2nd ed. Mahwah, NJ: Erlbaum, 2000. 559–591.

Rose, Mike. *Lives on the Boundary: The Struggles and Achievements of America's Underprepared.* New York: Free Press, 1989.

Rosenblatt, Abram, Jeff Greenberg, Sheldon Solomon, Tom Pyszczynski, and Deborah Lyon. 1989. "Evidence for Terror Management Theory I: The Effects of Mortality Salience on Reactions to Those Who Violate or Uphold Cultural Values." *Journal of Personality and Social Psychology* 57: 681–690.

Rossiter, Marsha. "A Narrative Approach to Development: Implications for Adult Education." *Adult Education Quarterly* 50.1 (Nov. 1999): 56–71,

Russo, Mary. "Aging and the Scandal of Anachronism." *Figuring Age: Women, Bodies, Generations.* Ed. Kathleen Woodward. Bloomington: Indiana UP, 1999.

Ryan, Ellen Bouchard, Sheree Kwong See, W. Bryan Meneer, and Diane Trovato. "Age-Based Perceptions of Conversational Skills Among Younger and Older Adults." *Interpersonal Communication in Older Adulthood: Interdisciplinary Theory and Research.* Eds. Mary Lee Hummert, John M. Wiemann, and Jon F. Nussbau. Thousand Oaks, CA: Sage, 1994, 15–39.

Ryan, Jake and Charles Sackery. *Strangers in Paradise: Academics Form [i.e. from] the Working Class.* Boston: South End P, 1984.

Salthouse, Timothy A. "Speed Mediation of Adult Age Differences in Cognition" *Developmental Psychology* 12(1993): 722–738.

Salthouse, Timothy A. "The Processing-Speed Theory of Adult Age Differences in Cognition." *Psychological Review* 103.3 (1996): 403–428.

Salthouse, Timothy A. and Sara J. Czaja. "Structural Constraints on Process Explanations in Cognitive Aging" *Psychology and Aging* 15.1 (2000): 44–55.

Sawchuck, Kimberly Anne. "From Gloom to Boom: Age, Identity and Target Marketing." *Images of Ageing: Cultural Representations of Later Life.* Ed. Mike Featherstone and Andrew Wernick. London: Routledge, 1995. 173–187.

Schell, Ellen E. *Gypsy Academics and Mother-Teachers: Gender, Contingent Labor, and Writing Instruction.* Portsmouth, NH: Boynton/Cook-Heinemann, 1998.

Schell, Ellen E. and Patricia Lambert Stock. *Moving a Mountain: Transforming the Role of Contingent Faculty in Composition Studies and Higher Education.* Urbana, IL: NCTE, 2001.

Schoenfeld, Clay A. and Robert Magnam. *Mentor in a Manual: Climbing the Academic Ladder to Tenure.* Madison, WI: Magna, 1994.

Scott, Jean Pearson: "Family Relationships of Midlife and Older Women." *Handbook on Women and Aging.* Ed. Jean M. Coyle. Westport, CT: Greenwood P, 1997. 367–383.

Sedgwick, Eve. *Tendencies.* Durham: Duke UP, 1993.

Selber, Stuart A., Johndan Johnson-Eilola, and Cynthia L. Selfe. "Contexts for Faculty Professional Development in the Age of Electronic Writing and Communication." *Technical Communication* 42.1 (Nov. 1995): 581–584.

Selfe, Cynthia L. "Preparing to Teach and Learn in Virtual Spaces: Ideas for Successful Faculty." Computers and Writing 2002. Illinois State University, Illinois, May 2002.

_____ . CCCC address, "College Composition and Communication Conference." Chicago, April 1998.

_____ . *Technology and Literacy in the Twenty-First Century: The Perils of Not Paying Attention*. Carbonale: Southern Illinois UP, 1999.

_____ . "To His Nibs, G. Douglas Atkins—Just in Case You're Serious about Your Not-So-Modest Proposal." *Journal of Advanced Composition* 20.2 (2000): 403–413.

Selfe, Cynthia L, Gail E. Hawisher, and Patty Ericsson. "Stasis and Change: The Role of Independent Composition Programs and the Dynamic Nature of Literacy." *A Field of Dreams: Independent Writing Programs and the Future of Composition Studies*. Eds. Peggy O'Neill, Angela Crow, and Larry Burton: Logan: Utah State UP, 2002.

Selfe, Cynthia and Susan Hilligoss, Eds. *Literacy and Computers: The Complications of Teaching and Learning with Technology*. New York: Modern Language Association, 1994.

Settersten, Richard A. and Gunhild O. Hagestad. "What's the Latest? Cultural Age Deadlines for Family Transitions." *The Gerontologist* 36.2 (1996): 178–188.

Settersten, Richard and Gunhild Hagestad. 1996. "What's the Latest? II. Cultural Age Deadlines for Educational and Work Transitions." *The Gerontologist* 36: 602–613.

Settersten, Richard A. Jr. and Loren D. Lovegreen. "Educational Experiences Throughout Adult Life: New Hopes or No Hope for Life-Course Flexibility?" *Research on Aging* 20.4 (1998): 506–538.

Shah, Priti and Akira Miyake. "Models of Working Memory, An Introduction." *Models of Working Memory: Mechanisms of Active Maintenance and Executive Control*. Eds. Akira Miyake and Priti Shah. Cambridge: Cambridge UP, 1999. 1–27.

Sherman, Susan R. "Images of Middle-Aged and Older Women: Historical, Cultural, and Personal." *Handbook on Women and Aging*. Ed. Jean M. Coyle. Westport, CT: Greenwood P, 1997. 14–28.

Shor, Ira. *When Students Have Power: Negotiating Authority in a Critical Pedagogy*. Chicago: U of Chicago P, 1996.

Sinnott, Jan D. "Developmental Models of Midlife and Aging in Women: Metaphors for Transcendence and for Individuality in Community. *Handbook on Women and Aging*. Ed. Jean M. Coyle. Westport, CT: Greenwood P, 1997. 149–163.

Smith, Michael W., Joseph Sharit, and Sara J. Czaja, "Aging, Motor Control, and the Performance of Computer Mouse Tasks." *Human Factors* 41: 389–396.

Smitherman, Geneva. *Talkin and Testifyin: The Language of Black America*. Boston: Houghton Mifflin, 1977. Reissued, with revisions, Detroit: Wayne State University Press, 1986.

Somers, Margaret. "The Narrative Construction of Identity: A Relational and Network Approach." *Theory and Society* 23: 605–649.

Sontag, Susan. "The Double Standard of Aging." *The Other Within Us: Feminist Explorations of Women and Aging*. Ed. Marilyn Pearsall. Boulder: Westview (HarperCollins), 1997. 19–24.

St. Clair, Ralf. "On the Commonplace: Reclaiming Community in Adult Education." *Adult Education Quarterly* 49.1 (Fall 1998): 5–14.

Stalker, Joyce. "Misogyny, Women, and Obstacles to Tertiary Education: A Vile Situation." *Adult Education Quarterly* 51.4 (Aug. 2001): 288–305.

Stine, Elizabeth A. L. "Aging and the Distribution of Resources in Working Memory." *Age Differences in Word and Language Processing.* Eds. Philip A. Allen and Theoder R. Bashore. New York: Elsevier, 1995. 171–186.

Street, Brian. *Social Literacies: Critical Approaches to Literacy in Development, Ethnography and Education.* London: Longman, 1995.

Strunk, William Jr., E. B. White, and Roger Angell. *Elements of Style.* 4th ed. New York: Longman, 2000.

Stuckey, Elspeth J. *The Violence of Literacy.* Portsmouth: Boynton/Cook, 1991.

Taylor, Denny. *Toxic Literacies: Exposing the Injustice of Bureaucratic Texts.* Portsmouth, NH: Heinemann, 1996.

Techrhet list. http://www.interversity.org/lists/techrhet/index.php (accessed June 1, 2004).

Thomas, Carol. "Narrative Identity and the Disabled Self." *Disability Discourse.* Eds. Mairian Corker and Sally French. Philadelphia: Open UP, 1999.

Tierney, William G. and Robert A. Rhoads. *Enhancing Promotion, Tenure and Beyond: Faculty Socialization as a Cultural Process.* Washington, DC: George Washington UP, 1994.

Tomlinson-Keasey, Carol and Jessica N. Gomel. "Antecedent Life Events and Consequences for Homemakers and Women Employed in Atypical, Typical, and Androgynous Professions. *Multiple Paths of Midlife Development.* Eds. Margie E. Lachman and Jacquelyn Boone James. Chicago: U of Chicago P, 1997.

Vandewater, Elizabeth A. and Abigail J. Stewart. "Women's Career Commitment Patterns and Personality Development." *Multiple Paths of Midlife Development.* Eds. Margie E. Lachman and Jacquelyn Boone James. Chicago: U of Chicago P, 1997. 375–410.

Van Hees, Maartje M. W. "User Instructions for the Elderly: What the Literature Tells Us." *Journal of Technical Writing and Communication* 26.4 (1996): 521–536.

Verillo, Ron T., and V. Verillo. "Sensory and Perceptual performance." *Aging and Human Performance.* Ed. N. Charness. New York: Wiley, 1985.

Villaneuva, Victor. *Bootstraps: From an American Academic of Color.* Urbana: NCTE, 1993.

Walker, Neff, Jeff Millians, and Aileen Worden. "Mouse Accelerations and Performance of Older Computer Users." *Proceedings of the Human Factors and Ergonomics Society 40th Annual Meeting. Philadelphia* 1 (1996): 151–154.

Walker, Neff, David A. Philbin, and Arthur D. Fisk. Age-Related Differences in Movement Control: Adjusting Submovement Structure to Optimize Performance. *Journal of Gerontology: Psychological Sciences,* 52B(1997): 40–52.

Wendell, Susan. *The Rejected Body: Feminist Philosophical Reflections on Disability* New York: Routledge, 1996.

Whitbourne, Susan Krauss and Joel R. Sneed. "The Paradox of Well-Being, Identity Processes, and Stereotype Threat: Ageism and Its Potential Relationships to the Self in Later Life. *Ageism: Stereotyping and Prejudice against Older Persons.* Ed. Todd D. Nelson. Cambridge, MA: MIT, 2002. 247 –273.

Williams, Patricia. *Seeing a Color-Blind Future: The Paradox of Race.* New York: Noonday, 1998.

Williams, David R. and Colwick M. Wilson. "Race, Ethnicity, and Aging." *Handbook of Aging and the Social Sciences.* Ed. Robert H. Binstock and Linda K. George. 5th edition. San Diego: Academic P, 2001. 160–178.

Woodward, Kathleen. "Introduction." *Figuring Age: Women, Bodies, Generations.* Ed. Kathleen Woodward. Bloomington: Indiana UP, 1999. ix–xxix.

Woodward. Kathleen "Against Wisdom: The Social Politics of Anger and Aging." *Journal of Aging Studies* 17 (2003): 55–67

Worden, Aileen, Neff Walker, Krishna Bharat, and Scott Hudson. "Making Computers Easier for Older Adults to Use: Area Cursors and Sticky Icons." *CHI Electronic Publications: Papers.* http://www.acm.org/sigchi/chi97/proceedings/paper/nw.htm (Jan 6, 2003)

WPA list discussions. http://lists.asu.edu/archives/wpa-l.html (accessed June 1, 2004)

Wright, Erik Olin. *Class Counts: Comparative Studies in Class Analysis* Cambridge, England: Cambridge UP, 1997.

Wyosocki, Anne. "Impossibly Distinct: On Form/Content and Word/Image in Two Pieces of Computer-Based Interactive Multimedia." *Computers & Composition* 18(2001): 137–162.

Wysocki, Anne and Johndan Johnson-Eilola. "Blinded by the Letter." *Passions, Pedagogies, and 21st Century Technologies.* Eds Gail E. Hawisher and Cynthia L. Selfe. Logan: Utah State UP, 1999. 349–368.

Yancey, Kathleen. "Keynote Address: Made Not Only in Words: Composition in a New Key." College Composition and Communication Conference. San Antonio, 2004.

Yeatts, Dale E., W. Edward Folts, and James Knapp. "Older Workers' Adaptation to a Changing Workplace: Employment Issues for the 21st century." *Educational Gerontology* 26 (2000): 565–582.

AUTHOR INDEX

SUBJECT INDEX

Printed in the United States
46375LVS00006B/205-228

9 781572 736436